THE MEANING OF LIFE

and other lectures on fundamental issues

Rudolf Steiner

translated by Johanna Collis

Mike Reiners
Feb. 5, 2002

RUDOLF STEINER PRESS
LONDON

Rudolf Steiner Press
51 Queen Caroline Street
London W6 9QL

First English edition 1999

Earlier English publications: lectures 1 & 2 in *On the Meaning of Life*,
Anthroposophical Publishing Co./Anthroposophic Press, London/New
York 1928; lectures 3 & 4 in *Illusory Illness and the Feverish Pursuit of Health*,
Anthroposophic Press, New York 1969; lecture 5 in *Good Fortune, Its
Reality and Semblance*, Anthroposophical Publishing Co., London 1956;
lecture 6, in *Spiritual Research, Methods and Results*, Steinerbooks, New
York 1981; lecture 7, *Some Characteristics of Today*, Sozialwissenschaftliche
Vereinigung am Goetheanum, Dornach, no date.

Originally published in German in various volumes of the GA (*Rudolf
Steiner Gesamtausgabe* or Collected Works) by Rudolf Steiner Verlag,
Dornach. Lectures 1 & 2 in GA 155; lectures 3 & 4 in GA 56; lecture 5 in
GA 61; lecture 6 in GA 168; lecture 7 in GA 193. This authorized
translation is published by kind permission of the Rudolf Steiner
Nachlassverwaltung, Dornach

Translation © Rudolf Steiner Press 1999

A catalogue record for this book is available from the British Library

ISBN 1 85584 092 8

Cover by Andrew Morgan
Typeset by DP Photosetting, Aylesbury, Bucks
Printed and bound in Great Britain by Cromwell Press Limited,
Trowbridge, Wilts.

Contents

Publisher's Note

The lectures collected together in this volume were given between the years 1907 and 1919. They were originally published in various volumes of Rudolf Steiner's collected works in German, and likewise in various English editions (see p. ii for further details). Most of the latter were in booklet form, and have been out of print for some years.

We are now taking the opportunity of publishing these popular lectures under one cover for the first time. Although they address questions as varied as reincarnation and psychological distress, they nevertheless share an overall common theme in that they all speak to practical and fundamental issues linked with modern life. As is evident from these lectures, Steiner's teaching is no tedious, abstract philosophy, but is vitally connected to the essential questions with which most people, whether consciously or not, struggle with today.

SG, London, June 1999

PART ONE:

THE MEANING OF LIFE

1. Growth, Decay and Reincarnation[1]

In these two evening lectures I should like to speak from the viewpoint of spiritual research about a question people ask frequently and urgently: 'What is the meaning of life?' Today we shall first lay a kind of foundation upon which we can then erect the edifice of knowledge that will outline a brief answer to our question—such as can be given in two evenings.

If we consider what is all around us—things that exist for our ordinary sense-perception and our ordinary experience, and which can be directly observed—and then turn to look at our own life, we can at best arrive at a question, a difficult and worrying question. We see how the creatures of external nature come into being and disappear again. Every year in spring we can observe how the earth, stimulated by the forces of sun and cosmos, presents us with plants that germinate and sprout, bearing their fruits throughout the summer. As autumn approaches, we see how these creations pass away. Some of course remain with us for several years, or for very many years, such as our long-lived trees. But even if these outlive us, we know that eventually they will pass away, disappear, sink down into that part of nature that is the lifeless realm. We know in particular that growth and decay rule everywhere even in the greatest phenomena of nature; we know that even the continents that provide a basis for our civilizations have not always existed. They have arisen in the course of time and we know for sure that one day they will once more fall in ruins.

All around us we see growth and decay. You can observe these processes in the plant and mineral kingdoms and also in the animal kingdom. So what is the meaning of it all? Wherever we look there is always something coming into being and something else fading away. What is the meaning of this becoming and this dying? Looking at our own life we find that over the years and decades we, too, have experienced growth and decay. Thinking of our early youth we find it has vanished, leaving only memories behind. These stir up anxious questions about our life. Having done one thing or another we ask: 'What did it lead to? What has come into being through my having done that thing?' The most important consequence is that we shall have progressed a little ourselves, that we shall have grown a little in wisdom. Usually, however, we only realize how we ought to have done things once we have done them. We only know how everything could have been done much better once we are no longer in a position to do it, so actually we do include in our life all the mistakes we have made. It is through these mistakes and errors that we gain our widest experiences.

A question confronts us, and it seems that what we grasp through our senses and comprehend with our understanding holds no answer for us. This is the position we human beings are in. Everything around us leads to the anxious question: 'What is the meaning of the whole of existence?' And to another question also: 'Why have we human beings been placed into this existence in the way we have?' This is the question confronting us.

A most interesting legend of Hebrew antiquity tells how in those old Hebrew times people knew that this anxious question about the meaning of life, and in our case the meaning of being human, occurs not only to humans but to other beings as well. The legend is most interesting and this is how it goes.

When the Elohim were preparing to create man in their own image and likeness, beings called ministering angels, spirits lower than the Elohim themselves, asked Yahveh or Jehovah: 'Why shall human beings be made in the image and likeness of God?' Then, so the legend continues, Yahveh gathered the animals and plants that had already sprung forth before man existed in his earthly form, and he also gathered the angels, the ministering angels, those in his immediate service. To these he showed the animals and plants, asking what they were called, what their names were. But the angels knew neither the names of the animals nor those of the plants. Then man was created as he was before the Fall. And again Jehovah or Yahveh gathered the angels, and also the animals and plants, and in the presence of the angels he asked man to name the names of the animals he caused to pass before him in procession. Lo and behold, man replied: 'This animal bears this name, and that animal that name; this plant bears this name and that plant that name.' Then Jehovah asked man: 'What is your own name?' And man replied: 'I must be called Adam.' (Adam is related to Adama, meaning: out of earthly slime, creature of earth.) And Jehovah asked man further: 'What shall I myself be called?' And man replied: 'You shall be called Adonai, you are lord of all created beings on the earth.' The angels now had an inkling of the meaning of man's existence on the earth.

Religious traditions and religious writings often express the most important of life's riddles in very simple terms, yet this does not mean there are no difficulties in understanding them, for we first have to find out what is hidden behind the simplicity. If we succeed in doing so, great wisdom and deep knowledge are revealed, as will indeed be the case with this legend. For the present we shall simply keep it in mind, for these two lectures are likely to give us some kind of answer to the questions it raises.

You know that there is a religion which has put the question as to the meaning and value of life by placing it in an over-whelmingly wonderful form into the very mouth of its founder. You all know the stories of Buddha that tell us of his departure from the palace in which he had been born. When he came face to face with the real facts of life, of which in that incarnation he had as yet learned nothing while still in the palace, he was profoundly dismayed about life and pronounced the judgement: 'Life is suffering'—which, as we know, encompasses four statements: 'Birth is suffering, illness is suffering, old age is suffering, death is suffering.' To these are added: 'To be united with those whom one does not love is suffering, to be parted from those whom one loves is suffering, not to achieve one's aim is suffering.' This tells us that for adherents of this religion the meaning of life can be encapsulated in the words: 'Life, which is suffering, is only meaningful if it can be overcome, if it can be transcended.'

Basically, all the various religions and also all philosophies and world views are attempts to answer the question: 'What is the meaning of life?' Rather than approach this question in a philosophically abstract manner, we shall here review some of the phenomena of life, some of the facts of life, from the point of view of spiritual science. We shall endeavour to look more deeply into these facts in order to discover whether a profounder, more spiritual view of life can come up with something approaching an answer regarding its meaning.

Let us begin again at the point we have already touched on, the annual growth and decay in sense-perceptible nature and life, growth and decay in the plant kingdom. In spring we see the plants sprouting up out of the ground, and this germinating, budding life calls forth our joy and delight. We become aware that the whole of our existence is bound up with the plant kingdom without which we could not exist. We sense that everything springing from the ground as summer approaches is related to our own life; and when autumn comes we feel those things that belong to us dwindling away again.

Naturally we compare our own life with the growth and decay we observe. For external observation based solely on what can be perceived by the senses and judged by the intellect it would be quite natural to compare the vernal sprouting of the plants out of the ground with our waking up in the morning, and the autumnal withering and fading of the plants with our going to sleep in the evening. But such a comparison would be entirely superficial in that it leaves out of account what actually happens according to even the more elementary truths of spiritual science. What does happen when we go to sleep at night? We know that we leave our physical body and ether body behind in bed while our astral body and 'I' withdraw from them. During the night, between going to sleep and waking up, we live in a world of spirit with our astral body and 'I'. From this world of spirit we gather the forces we need. As well as our astral body and 'I', our physical body and ether body also undergo a kind of restorative process, a regeneration, as they lie in bed separated from the other two during our night-time sleep.

Looking clairvoyantly down from 'I' and astral body to ether and physical body, we can see what has been destroyed by our daytime life; we see that what expresses itself as tiredness is in fact destruction, and that this is restored during the night. The whole phenomenon of human consciousness and the way it relates to physical and ether body is seen as a process that is destructive for physical and ether body. We destroy something with our consciousness, and the fact of this destruction manifests as tiredness. What we have destroyed is restored again during the night.

What we see when we have departed from ether body and

physical body with our astral body and 'I' resembles a field laid waste. But the moment we have gone this field begins to regenerate. It is as though the forces belonging to the physical and ether bodies were beginning to flower and sprout, as if a whole vegetation were rising from the devastation. The further the night advances, the longer we sleep, the more does the sprouting and springing up continue in our ether body. The closer we get to morning, the more we enter our physical and ether bodies with our astral body, the more does a kind of wilting and withering begin again in our physical and ether bodies.

In short, when 'I' and astral body look down on our physical and our ether body as we go to sleep at night, what they see is the same manifestation as that confronting us in the great world outside us when the plants spring up and sprout in springtime. Thus the comparison we must draw on a more intimate level likens our going to sleep and the beginning of our sleeping state at night with springtime in nature, and our waking up, when our 'I' and astral body re-enter our physical and ether bodies, with autumn in nature. This, not the opposite, is the correct comparison to draw. The opposite is a superficial comparison. In human beings springtime corresponds to falling asleep and autumn to waking up.

How does the matter stand when a clairvoyant observer, someone who can truly look into the spiritual world, turns his attention to external nature and watches what goes on there in the course of the year? The clairvoyant view teaches us to compare things in an inward, not an outward, way. With clairvoyant vision we see that just as the physical and ether bodies of the human being are joined with astral body and 'I', so is the earth joined with what we can call its spiritual aspect. The earth, too, is a body, a vast body, and looking only at its physical part is like taking only the human physical body into account. To see the earth in its completeness we have to regard it as the body of spiritual beings, just as with the human being we see the spirit as belonging to the body. There is one difference, however. Man is a single being governing his physical and etheric bodies. A single soul-and-spirit corresponds to the human physical and etheric body. But the earth's body has a great many spirits belonging to it. The soul-and-spiritual element in man is a unity, whereas for the earth it is a multiplicity. This is the most obvious distinction.

Having accepted this difference, we shall find everything else more or less analogous. Spiritual vision sees that in spring the earth spirits depart from the earth to the same degree as the plants grow up from the ground and greenery spreads, although it is not quite the same as with the human being, for rather than departing entirely, as is the case with the human spirit, the earth spirits redistribute themselves; they move round to the opposite side of the globe. When it is summer in one hemisphere it is winter in the other. As summer comes to the northern hemisphere, the spirit-and-soul part of the earth moves from the northern to the southern hemisphere. This does not alter the fact that a clairvoyant person anywhere on the globe sees the spirits of the earth departing when he experiences the coming of spring; he sees how they rise up and pass out into the cosmos. Rather than seeing them move to the other side he sees them departing, just as he sees the 'I' departing with the astral body when a human being falls asleep. The clairvoyant sees the spirits of the earth going away from that with which they have been bound up, whereas in winter, while the ground was covered in ice and snow, the spiritual forces were united with the earth. In the autumn the opposite takes place when clairvoyant vision sees the earth spirits approaching and reuniting with the earth. Something then begins for the earth that resembles what takes place in man—a kind of self-awareness. In summer the spiritual part of the earth knows nothing of what is going on around it in the cosmos. But in winter the spirit of the earth does know what is going on around it in the cosmos, just as the human being, on waking up, sees and knows what is going on around him. The analogy is entirely valid, only it is the reverse of the conclusion drawn by external consciousness.

There is something that must be added, however, in order to complete the picture. It is true to say that the earth spirits depart when the plants sprout and burst forth from the earth in spring. In fact, other more mighty spirits then rise up as though out of the depths, out of the interior of the earth. The mythologies were right to distinguish between the higher and the nether gods, and when people spoke of the gods who leave the earth in spring and return in the autumn they meant the higher gods. But there are mightier, older gods called by the Greeks the chthonian gods who rise up when everything buds and sprouts in summer and sink down again in winter when the real earth spirits unite once more with the body of the earth.

These are the facts, and I should now like to mention a certain idea taken from spiritual research into nature that is of immense importance for our lives. This research shows that an individual human being presents us with an image of the great earth being. What do we see in the plants as they begin to bud and sprout? We see exactly what the human being does inwardly while asleep. The one corresponds exactly with the other. How individual plants are related to the human body, what their significance is for the human body, can only be recognized when such connections are understood. If you watch closely as a human being goes to sleep you see how everything begins to bud and sprout in his physical body and his etheric body; you see a whole vegetation spring up, or that the human being is actually a tree, or a garden with plants growing in it.

If you follow this with clairvoyant vision you see how the sprouting and budding within the human being corresponds to the sprouting and budding in outer nature. This gives us an idea of what may come about in future when spiritual science—which is for the most part still regarded as nonsense—is applied to life and made fruitful. Suppose a person has something wrong in the external life functions of his body. You can observe this person asleep and see which plant species are missing when his physical and ether bodies begin to unfold their vegetation. When we notice that whole species of plant are absent at some location on the earth, we know that there is something not quite right with the life of the earth there. It is the same when certain plants are missing in the person's physical and ether body. In order to remedy the deficiency in the person we need only seek out the missing plants in nature and apply their juices in a suitable form, either in the diet or medicinally. Then, out of their inner forces, we shall discover the relationship between medicine and illness. This shows us one way in which spiritual science will intervene directly in life, although at present we are only at the beginning of these things.

With this image I have given you a basic truth about nature concerning the way the human being is related with his whole being to the surroundings in which he finds himself.

Let us now look at the matter from a spiritual point of view, and in doing so I would like to call attention to something rather important. In its endeavours to discover the meaning of life, spiritual science encompasses the whole range of human evolution from the spiritual point of view without according any outer preference to one particular world view or creed over another. Within our stream of spiritual wisdom we have often described what earthly humanity developed and experienced immediately after the great Atlantean catastrophe.[2] The first great post-Atlantean culture we come across in doing this is the ancient sacred culture of India. Here in Copenhagen we have spoken about this too, stressing the exaltedness of this culture by pointing out that the Vedas or other extant written traditions are merely echoes of it. Only in the Akashic Record can we catch a glimpse of the primeval teachings that issued from that time.[3] There we discover a loftiness of culture never since regained.

The subsequent epochs of culture have quite other tasks. We also know that a descent has taken place since those times, that there will be a new ascent and, as we have already said, that spiritual science exists in order to prepare for this ascent. We know that in the seventh post-Atlantean culture there will be a kind of renewal of the ancient sacred Indian civilization. In this sense we give no preference to any religious view or creed. The same yardstick is applied to each one, each is described in detail and the core of truth in all of them is sought.

The important thing is to keep the essentials in view. We must not allow ourselves to stray off course as we consider the core of every religious creed, and if we keep this in mind in approaching the various world views we discover one fundamental difference. We discover that there are world views of a more oriental nature, and others that have imbued the culture of the West. Having made this quite clear to ourselves we find that it throws a great deal of light on the meaning of existence. We discover that the ancients had something which we shall have to make great efforts to regain, namely, teachings about reincarnation. The oriental streams possessed this knowledge as something springing from the profoundest depths of life. You can still see how those oriental streams modelled their whole life from this point of view when you observe the relationship oriental people have with their bodhisattvas and their buddhas. If you keep in view how disinclined oriental people are to select a single figure with this or that definite name as the ruling power in human evolution, you see at once how they attach much greater importance to tracing the individuality who goes on from one life to the next.

Orientalists say that there are such and such a number of bodhisattvas, high beings who sprang from mankind and then evolved to an exaltedness we can describe by saying that a being has lived through many incarnations and has then become a bodhisattva—as did Gautama, the son of King Suddhodana. Having been a bodhisattva he became a buddha. Many are given the name of buddha after having lived through numerous incarnations to become a bodhisattva and thereafter reaching the next stage, that of a buddha. Buddha is a general designation. It denotes a degree of human attainment and is meaningless when no account is taken of the being of spirit and soul who has lived through many incarnations. Brahmanism fully agrees with Buddhism in placing greater importance on the individual being who is the continuing element in many successive personalities, rather than on single personalities. It amounts to the same thing whether a Buddhist says: 'A bodhisattva is destined to rise to the highest possible degree of human attainment for which he must live through many incarnations; and for me the highest is the Buddha,' or whether an adherent of Brahmanism says: 'Bodhisattvas are highly evolved beings who ascend to buddhahood; they stem from the Avatars, those higher spiritual individualities.' Both these oriental points of view share the recognition of a spiritual entity who lives through many incarnations.

Let us now look to the West and see who are the great and

mighty there. To go more deeply into this we have to consider the ancient Hebrew point of view and look at the personal element. When we speak of Plato, Socrates, Michelangelo, Charlemagne or others, we always mean a person; we point to the finite life of a personality and what that personality did for humanity. In western culture we do not look for a life that has moved on from person to person, for it has been the task of western culture to pay attention for a time to the single life on earth. When a buddha is spoken of in the East, people know that this designates a title covering many personalities. But to name Plato is to designate a single personality. This has been the education in the West, where for a while the personal element had to be esteemed and respected.

What is the appropriate attitude in our own time to this sequence of facts? For a while, western culture has trained humanity to pay attention to the personality. But now the time has come to conjoin the individual, the individuality, with the personal. We must reconquer the individual element, strengthened now, enlivened by contemplation of the personal.

Let us take a specific case and in doing so begin by looking towards the ancient Hebrew world view that preceded the western outlook. Consider a mighty personality such as the prophet Elijah. Initially we shall describe him as a personality, for in the West he is seldom regarded in any other way. Leaving details aside and looking at the personality overall, we see Elijah as being very important in world evolution. He expresses something that resembles being a forerunner of the Christ-impulse.

Looking back to the time of Moses we find something being foretold to the people, we see the God in man being proclaimed: 'I, the God, who was, who is and who shall be.' In the 'I' he must be comprehended, and among the ancient

Hebrews he was comprehended as the soul of the people. Elijah went beyond this. He did not yet make it clear that the 'I' lives in the single human individuality as the highest spark of divinity, for he could not make clear to the people of his time more than the world was ready to receive. Nevertheless, a step further was taken in evolution. Whereas the Mosaic culture of the old Hebrews made it clear that the Highest lies in the 'I'—with this 'I' being expressed as the Folk Soul in the Moses age—we find Elijah beginning to point to the individual soul. A further incentive was needed for this, and again we find a kind of forerunner in the personality of John the Baptist. John the Baptist, too, expressed his function as a forerunner in significant words. What do these words mean? They give expression to an important occult fact, namely, that primeval human beings possessed an ancient clairvoyance which enabled them to look into the spiritual world, into divine activity. Then, however, they turned more towards the material world; they could no longer see into the spiritual world. John the Baptist pointed to this when he said: 'Change the attitude of your soul! Look no longer to what you can gain in the physical world! Be watchful: a new impulse'—he meant the Christ-impulse—'is at hand! Therefore I say to you: Seek the spiritual world in your very midst!' We see the spiritual world entering with the Christ-impulse, and with these words John the Baptist became the forerunner of the Christ-impulse.

Let us now turn our attention to another personality, the remarkable personality of the painter Raphael,[4] a personality who appears most unusual to us. Compare Raphael, a painter of the Latin people, with later painters, Titian, for example.[5] If you have an eye for such things you will soon discover the difference even if you have only reproductions at your disposal. Look at Raphael's and Titian's paintings. In the way he painted, Raphael put Christian ideas into his pictures. He painted for European people as western Christians. His pictures are comprehensible to all western Christians, and they will become even more so as time goes on. Compare this with the later painters who painted almost exclusively for peoples of the Latin race, so that even the schisms of the Church found expression in their pictures.

Which were Raphael's most successful paintings? They were the ones in which he was able to proclaim the incentives that are inherent in Christianity. He is at his best where he succeeds in representing the Jesus Child in his relationship with the Madonna, where he can present the relationship of Christ to the Madonna as an impulse of feeling. These are the things he painted best. We do not have a *Crucifixion* by him, for example, but there is a *Transfiguration*. Wherever he could paint the budding, germinating aspect, things that are to be proclaimed, there he painted with joy and made his greatest and best pictures.

It is the same with the effect his pictures produce. Perhaps you can go to Germany some day and see the *Sistine Madonna* in Dresden. The Germans may rejoice to have such a significant painting in their midst, one that is the flower of the painter's art. When you see it you will find that it reveals a mystery of existence.

What Goethe heard about the painting of the Madonna when he went from Leipzig to Dresden was rather different. Officials at the Dresden gallery said something like this: 'One of the pictures we have is by Raphael but it's nothing special; it's badly painted; the child's glance, in fact the whole of the child, everything about it, is common; the same has to be said of the Madonna; you have to assume that a dauber painted her; and as for those figures at the bottom, you can't tell whether they are meant to be children's heads or angels!' This is the uncouth opinion Goethe heard at that time, so at first he failed to appreciate the picture properly. Everything we now hear about the picture did not become common currency until later, but once that new appreciation had been reached copies of Raphael's paintings began their triumphal march around the globe. Think what England in particular has done for the reproduction and circulation of Raphael's pictures. However, the efforts made in England for the reproduction and circulation of Raphael's paintings will only be recognized when people have learnt to look at these things more from the point of view of spiritual science.

In this way Raphael is like an early foreteller of a Christianity that will be world-wide. Suspicious Protestantism long regarded the Madonna as something specifically Catholic. But today the Madonna has made her way into all the Protestant countries too, as we rise to a more spiritual interpretation, a higher, interdenominational Christianity. This will be the case more and more, and if we may hope for such results in the realm of interdenominational Christianity, what Raphael has done will also help us in spiritual science.

Remarkably, we have now met with three personalities, all of them having the quality of being forerunners of Christianity. So let us look at them with spiritual vision. What does it teach us? Spiritual vision teaches us that the same individuality lived in Elijah, in John the Baptist and in Raphael. Impossible though this may seem, it was the same soul who lived in Elijah, in John the Baptist and in Raphael.

In using spiritual vision we conduct research as opposed to making superficial, theoretical comparisons. This research having shown that the same soul existed in Elijah, John the Baptist and Raphael, we now have to ask: 'How can it be that the painter Raphael became the bearer of the individuality who had lived in John the Baptist? Can we imagine that the remarkable soul of John the Baptist lived in the forces present in Raphael?'

Again we apply spiritual research not merely to set up theories but to describe things as they really are in life. How do people write biographies of Raphael today? Even the best make nothing special of the fact that he was born on Good Friday in 1483. Yet it is not for nothing that Raphael was born on a Good Friday. Even this very date of birth proclaims his special position in Christianity, showing how profoundly and meaningfully he is connected with the mysteries of Christianity.

It was on a Good Friday that Raphael was born. His father was Giovanni Santi who died when the boy was eleven years old.[6] When he was eight his father had apprenticed him to a painter who was, however, not of any special eminence. When you realize what lived in Giovanni Santi, Raphael's father, you get a particular impression that is further strengthened by research into the Akashic Record. There you find that much more lived in the soul of Giovanni Santi than he was able to express, so we can agree with the words the duchess spoke when he died: 'A man full of light and truth and purest faith has died.' As a spiritual researcher one can say that a far greater painter lived in Giovanni Santi than was able to come to outward expression. His outer capabilities, those dependent on his physical and etheric organs, were underdeveloped. That was why the capabilities of his soul were unable to come to full expression although a really great painter lived in his soul.

He died when Raphael was eleven years old. When we follow up what this involved, we see how true it is that although a human being's body is lost his longings, the aspirations and motivations of his soul continue to exist, continue to work where their closest connections are.

A time will come when spiritual science will be made fruitful for life in the way those can already make it fruitful whose understanding for it is alive rather than theoretical. I should like to interpolate something here before continuing with Raphael. The examples I give do not involve speculation. On the contrary, they are always taken directly from life. Suppose you have children to bring up. If you watch their capabilities you soon discover the individual qualities in each child, but to notice such things you have to be the one bringing them up. If a child's mother or father dies early, leaving only one parent behind, you notice that after a while certain inclinations show themselves that were not there before and which are thus difficult to explain. As a teacher you have to concern yourself with such things, and the teacher would do well to disregard the way many people consider the content of anthroposophical books as foolish and instead keep an open mind about them. Then he would be willing to see whether what they contain might be right after all. With this attitude he would soon discover how new forces are entering those the child already had. Suppose the father has gone through the gate of death, and now characteristics that lived in him begin to come through fairly strongly in the child. (With the assumptions arising out of anthroposophy you can apply the knowledge it gives in a sensible way, soon discovering that you can find your way in life, whereas before you could not.) So, the one who has gone through the gate of death remains united in his forces with those who were close to him in life. People do not observe things thoroughly enough, otherwise they would notice how different children are before the death of their parents and how much they change afterwards. Not enough attention is paid to these things, but a time will come when people do pay more attention to them.

Giovanni Santi, the father, died when Raphael was eleven

years old. He had been unable to achieve any special perfection as a painter but that powerful imagination remained his own and this now entered the soul of Raphael and developed there. We do not depreciate or belittle Raphael if we say of his soul that Giovanni Santi lived on in Raphael. It is because of this that Raphael appears to us as one whose personality has reached completion; he appears as one incapable of going any further because a man who has died gives life to his works.

Since the energies of John the Baptist were reborn in the soul of the human being Raphael, and since in addition to these the energies of Giovanni Santi also lived in his soul, we now understand that these two together were able to bring into being the result that confronts us as Raphael.

It is not yet appropriate to speak publicly about such extraordinary things. Perhaps it will be appropriate in 50 years' time, for evolution is progressing quickly and current attitudes are rapidly approaching their decline. Those who look into these things will find that in spiritual science it is our task to inspect every aspect of life from a new angle. Just as in future healing will take the form I have hinted at, so will people reflect on the strange miracles of life by drawing on the help of deeds that come out of the spiritual world from human beings who have gone through the gate of death.

While I am on the subject of the riddles of life I should like to draw your attention to two more things, things that can most truly illustrate the meaning of life. One is the fate that is befalling the works of Raphael. When you look at reproductions of his pictures today you are not seeing what he painted. The same will apply if you go to Dresden or Rome, for the originals, too, have already deteriorated so much that you cannot really claim to be seeing the works of Raphael any longer. It is easy to see what will become of them when you consider the fate of Leonardo da Vinci's *Last Supper*, which is increasingly falling into disrepair. Obviously over time these pictures will fall to dust; sad to say, everything great people have ever created will disappear. Since these things are doomed to vanish we might enquire after the meaning of their creation and decay, and we shall see that nothing remains of what a single personality creates.

The other fact I should like to put before you is this. If we are to grasp Christianity today by using spiritual science as a tool—Christianity as a stimulus that works for the future, as I have already explained—then we shall need certain basic concepts through which we can know how the Christ-impulse will continue to work. We need these concepts. It may seem strange to be confronted by the fact that with the help of spiritual science we can point to a further development of Christianity. This involves a personality whose work expresses the truths of spiritual science in a particular form, that of the aphorism. When we approach this personality we find in him much that is significant for spiritual science. He is the German poet Novalis.[7] A study of his writings reveals that he can describe the future of Christianity out of the spiritual truths it contains. And spiritual science teaches us that his is the same individuality, the individuality of Raphael, John the Baptist and Elijah.

Once again we are given a foretelling of Christianity's further evolution. This is an occult fact, for no one can arrive at it by ordinary processes of reasoning.

Let us compare the different images once again. There is the tragic ruin of the creations and works of single personalities. Raphael appears and sends his interdenominational Christianity streaming into human souls. Yet we have the foreboding that his works will one day fall to dust. Then Novalis appears in order to take in hand once more the fulfilment of the task and continue the work Raphael has begun.

So now the idea is no longer so tragic, for we see that although the personality in all its aspects dissolves, and although the works created also dissolve, the core of being lives on and carries further what it once began. Our attention is directed yet again to the individuality. The significance of the individuality is now all the clearer to us because hitherto we have so energetically supported the western world view and paid attention only to the personality. We realize how significant it is that the Orient paid attention to the individuality and the bodhisattvas who go through very many incarnations, and how significant it is that the West first turned its attention to the single personality prior to reaching an understanding of the individuality.

There are probably many anthroposophists who will simply feel they have to accept what they are told about Elijah, and about John the Baptist, Raphael and Novalis. Many will have to take it on trust, just as most of us take on trust scientific statements about the spectral analysis of some metal or other, or of the Orion nebula. Some people have certainly made the investigation themselves, but the others, the majority, have to believe what they are told. But this is not the essential point. The main thing is that spiritual science is now at the beginning of its development and will bring more and more souls to the point of examining for themselves such matters as we have discussed today. In this respect, spiritual science will take human evolution forward very rapidly.

I have suggested a few aspects arising from the angle by which spiritual science approaches life. Take only the three points we have examined. You will see that through understanding the way in which life is related to the spirit of the earth the art of healing can be given a new direction and a new stimulus, and that Raphael can only be understood properly when not only the forces of his own personality are taken into account but also those forces that came from his father. The third point is that we can bring up children when we know how things stand in regard to the forces that come into play in them.

People are quite happy to admit that outwardly they are surrounded by countless forces which incessantly influence them, that they are constantly influenced by atmosphere, temperature and other climatic factors in their environment, and we all know that these things do not interfere with our freedom. These factors are already taken into account today. That we are also permanently surrounded by spiritual forces, and that these, too, deserve to be investigated, is something that spiritual science will teach us. We shall learn to reckon with these forces, especially in important situations regarding health and illness, education and life. We shall have to take into consideration the influences that come from our sur-roundings, from the spiritual world around us when, for example, a friend of ours dies and we find ourselves pre-occupied with some of the sympathies and ideas that had been close to that friend's heart. This applies not only to children but also to adults of all ages. Even if people do not realize with their daytime consciousness how the forces of the super-sensible world are at work in them, their general frame of mind can show this to be the case, as can their state of health or illness.

Indeed, the link between human beings in their life on the physical plane and the facts of the supersensible world can be followed even further. Let me show you a simple fact that will demonstrate this link, one that is not invented but has been observed in many cases.

At a specific point in time a person begins to notice that he has feelings different from those he is used to, and sympathies and antipathies he never had before, or that he can now do things easily that were formerly difficult for him. He has no explanation for this, and neither have those around him. Even the facts of his life provide no clue. When we observe such a person accurately—and one needs to have an eye for such things—we shall discover that he now knows things and can do things that he did not know before and could not do before. If we examine things further and have had experience of the teachings of spiritual science, we shall hear something like the following from him: 'I feel remarkably strange; I keep dreaming of someone I have never met in my life, someone who keeps coming into my dreams although I have never concerned myself with him.' When we pursue the matter further we find that hitherto he has had no occasion to concern himself with that person. But the person has now died and has begun to approach him in the spiritual world. Having become sufficiently close to him, the person then even shows himself in the shape of a dream that is more than a dream. The motivations in him that did not exist earlier are coming from that person whom he did not know during his lifetime but who, having died, has now gained some influence in his life.

Rather than simply maintaining that this is nothing but a dream, the important thing is to see what it signifies. Something may quite possibly appear in the form of a dream yet in fact be closer to reality than our external consciousness. Does it matter whether Edison made an invention in a dream or with his daytime consciousness? What matters is whether the invention is true and serviceable. In the same way the important thing is not whether an experience takes place in dream consciousness or in external, physical consciousness, but whether the experience is true or not.

Let us summarize what has been clarified in our considerations. We have come to understand that if we apply spiritual science to it, life reveals itself in quite a different light.

In this respect people who are very learned in materialistic ways of thinking are rather odd fish, as we can see at almost any time. On my way here in the train today I was reading a pamphlet by a German physiologist that has just been published in its second edition.[8] The writer maintains that there is no such thing as 'active attentiveness' in the soul, no way of directing one's soul towards anything, but that everything depends on the functioning of the different ganglia in the brain; since the tracks have to be followed by the thoughts, everything depends on how the individual brain cells function. He says that no intensity of soul, however strong, can intervene and that everything depends simply on whether one connecting link or another has been set up in our brain. These learned materialists really are oddly childish.

When you happen on statements like these you cannot help thinking how half-baked these people are. The same pamphlet mentions the fact that the centenary of Darwin's birth has recently been celebrated and that both qualified and unqualified people spoke at the ceremony. The writer of the pamphlet of course regards himself as one of those particularly qualified to speak. Then follows the whole brain-cell theory and its application. But where is the logic in all this?

If you are used to considering things in their true light and then see what these grown-up children have to offer us concerning the meaning of life, you cannot help thinking that their claims amount to the same as saying it is nonsense to assert that human will has had any influence on the way the railway system has been laid down across the face of Europe. This would be similar to taking all the engines in their parts and functions at the same moment and claiming that every engine has one function or another and runs in one direction or another, but since all the directions meet at certain intersections all the engines can potentially be diverted to run in any direction. The result would be a huge muddle of engines and trains on European railway lines. It is just as nonsensical to claim that the life of thought in the human being taking place in the cells of the brain depends entirely on the condition of the cells.

When learned gentlemen of this type stumble unprepared upon a lecture about spiritual science, they consider what they hear to be the most hopeless nonsense. They are firmly convinced that human will-power can never have anything to do with the mode in which European engines run; they are sure that everything depends on how they are stoked up and driven.

This is how the question about the meaning of life comes before us nowadays. On the one hand it is entirely obscured, while on the other the spiritual facts press in on us. Bringing together what we have been considering today we can use it as a basis for asking the question in a manner that befits spiritual science: 'What is the meaning of life and existence and especially of human life and human existence?'

2. Human Participation in Evolution[1]

It would be a serious mistake to imagine that having posed a simple question—'What is the meaning of life and existence?'—we might then expect to find someone able to supply a simple answer in a few words, such as: 'This (or that) is the meaning of life and existence.' No conception could ever be gained in this way that could do justice to the grandeur, majesty and power that lie hidden behind this question.

It is true that an abstract reply might be given, but you will sense from what I shall be saying later how unsatisfactory this would be. You might say: 'The meaning of life is that the spiritual beings to whom we look up as divinities shall gradually permit human beings to share in bringing about the evolution of existence, so that these human beings, initially imperfect and incapable of playing a part in the whole building of the universe, could, as they evolved, gradually be trained to share in this work of evolution.'

This would be an abstract reply, telling us very little indeed. What we need to do in order to gain even an inkling of a reply to such a far-reaching question is immerse ourselves in certain secrets of existence and life. So let us embark on some considerations on the basis of those we went into yesterday, and in this way penetrate a little further into the secrets of existence. Observing the world around us, it is not really enough merely to note the phenomena of growth and decay. We noticed yesterday how mysteriously growth and decay touch our soul when we enquire after their meaning. But there is something else that poses an even more difficult riddle.

As we look more closely at growth and decay things get even more mysterious. In growth itself, in the way creatures come into being, we discover something strange that gives us a feeling of sadness and tragedy when we look at it only superficially. We know from science that in the widths of the ocean, or indeed in any other medium of existence, countless seeds are sown, countless spawn come into being that never develop into fully matured creatures. Think how many eggs the various fish species lay in the sea each year that disappear before ever reaching their goal of becoming fully grown creatures; think how relatively few of those eggs reach the goal of becoming creatures.

Yesterday we saw how everything that comes into existence has to perish. Today this other fact is forcing itself on our attention, namely, that in the immeasurable realm of uncountable possibilities only a few realities materialize. So even in the origin of things there is something enigmatic in the way what strives to come to birth cannot really begin to come into being.

Look at a specific case, a wheat-field with myriads of ears of wheat. We know very well that out of every grain in those ears of wheat a new ear can come into existence. How many of all those grains in that field will actually achieve this potential? Think of the numberless grains that go in a direction quite different from their object of becoming ears of wheat in their turn. This is a specific example that can stand for all the other potential sources of life. We cannot help saying that the life surrounding us only comes into being in that it appears to plunge numberless potential life sources into an abyss of non-fulfilment.

Keep in mind the fact that what exists in our surroundings rises from a bed of infinitely rich potential that never becomes reality in the ordinary sense of the word. Keep in mind the way the realities arise from this soil and think of this as one side of the mysterious existence of life that our eyes see.

Let us now turn to the other side of the picture which also exists but of which we only become aware once we enter more deeply into spiritual truths. The other side is the one that opens up when we follow the path to spiritual knowledge. As you know, this path to spiritual knowledge is sometimes described as dangerous. Why? For the simple reason that when we follow the path to spiritual knowledge we enter a realm that cannot as a matter of course be accepted in the form in which we encounter it.

Suppose someone follows the spiritual path with the means known to him—which you may find in my book *Knowledge of the Higher Worlds*[2]—and reaches the point at which imaginations, as we call them, rise up from the depths of his soul.[3] We know what images these are. They are visionary images that come to meet someone who has trodden the spiritual path, images of a world entirely new to him. Someone treading this spiritual path with true seriousness reaches a point when the whole physical world around him grows dim. In place of this physical world there arises a world of surging images, impressions of a kind that are like sound, smell, taste, light. This world presses and whirls into our field of spirit vision, and we have experiences that we call experiences of Imagination which then surround us on all sides, and which are the world in which we live and weave with our soul.

If we were to be convinced that the visionary world we enter in this way is something entirely real, we should be making a serious, a very serious mistake, for this is the point where the danger begins. The visionary world conjured up for us by Imagination remains immeasurable unless we ascend to Inspiration. It is Inspiration that tells us the direction in which we must turn with our spirit vision in order to experience a truth; all the countless other images surrounding us have to disappear into the nothingness of non-existence. This one image that emerges from the numberless others will prove itself to be an expression of the truth.

Treading the spiritual path, we enter a realm of countless possible visions and must therefore develop the ability to set aside the countless other images and choose only those that truly express a spiritual reality. No other guarantee is possible than the one just mentioned. You might say: 'In the realm that is infinitely rich in visions, which are true and which are false? Can you not give me a rule by which I can separate the true from the false?' But no spiritual researcher would reply to this question by telling you a rule. Instead he would have to say: 'If you want to learn how to make the distinction you must go on developing yourself; then you, too, will find it possible to select those images that stand firm for you; those that stand firm for you are the ones that are compatible with your point of view, whereas those that you extinguish are merely secondary appearances.'

The danger lies in the fact that many people feel exceptionally comfortable and cosy in the realm of visions and are therefore reluctant to develop further and go on striving, since this visionary realm pleases them so much. You cannot attain reality in spiritual life if you simply succumb to this bliss and merely revel in that visionary world. Doing this prevents you from attaining reality or truth. You must go on striving with all the means in your power, for then what is spiritually real will separate out from the immeasurable sea of visions.

Let us now compare the two things I have described. On the one hand there is the outside world that generates countless possibilities of life but only permits a few to reach maturity; on the other hand there is the inner world to which we are led by the path of knowledge: an immeasurable world of visions comparable to that outer world with its limitless potential for life. We end up with only a few of the visions, which may be compared with the relatively few real lives that emerge from among the many possibilities. These two things correspond exactly; they belong together entirely in the world.

We can now take this thought a little further by asking: 'Is it right to be despondent and sad about life and existence because this life only allows that huge potential to come into being partially, letting only a few seeds reach their goal? Is it possible for us to be sad about this, describing the whole as a wild struggle for survival from which only a few escape by accident?' Consider the example of the wheat-field. Suppose every single grain coming into being there were to achieve its goal and become a new ear of wheat. What would be the consequence? The world would be impossible, since the animals for whom the grains provide nourishment would have no food. For the animals familiar to us to reach their present stage of evolution, those other living things have to fall short of their goal, they have to sink into the abyss in so far as achieving their own goal is concerned. So we have no reason to be sad, unless the world means nothing at all to us. If it does mean something to us, and since it consists entirely of created beings, we have to allow for these creatures to have the possibility of finding food. If they are to find food, others must sacrifice themselves. Therefore only a few potential living beings can reach their final goal while the others must go another way. They must go another way because the world has to remain in existence, since this is really the only manner in which the world can be wisely ordered.

We are, then, only surrounded by a world such as ours because certain creatures sacrifice themselves before they achieve their potential. If we follow the path taken by the ones that have sacrificed themselves, we find them in the other creatures, in the higher ones, the ones who need the sacrifice in order to exist. We have thus managed to grasp one corner, you might say, of the meaning of this seemingly so mysterious existence which can come into being and yet also sink into nothingness. We have also discovered that wisdom is revealed in this, that meaning is revealed, and that if we lament about so much having to sink down into the abyss in such a seemingly pointless fashion it is in our thinking that we are being too short-sighted.

Let us now go once more to the other side, the spiritual side, and look at what we called the immeasurable world of visions. We shall have to enter into the meaning of this immeasurable world of visions. It is not simply wrong in the sense of saying that what falls away is wrong, while what finally remains is right. That world is not wrong in this sense. This judgement is just as short-sighted as would be the statement that the seeds which do not reach their goal are not proper seeds, or the Imaginations that from our point of view disappear into infinity are not real Imaginations. In the same way that in real external life only a few creatures achieve their potential, so can only a small part of immeasurable spiritual life enter our horizons. Why?

Answering this question will teach us a great deal. Suppose someone were to surrender himself entirely to the immeasurable variety of visions streaming in on him. A person for whom the visionary world has opened up is filled with a continual stream of visions; one after another they come and go and surge and flow into one another. It is impossible to shut yourself off from these images and impressions that pulsate and surge in the spiritual world.

On closer inspection we find something very peculiar in a person who thus simply surrenders himself to this visionary world. When we encounter someone who does not want to develop any further but would rather remain in the visionary realm, we discover, firstly, that perhaps he has had an experience of some kind. 'Very well,' we say, 'you have had spiritual experiences, you have experienced things that are real to you; fine, that is a manifestation of the spiritual world.' But when we meet someone else who is no more developed than the other, we soon find that what he tells us about his visions concerning the same subject is quite different. So we can have two differing statements about the same subject.

But things can get worse still. We discover that people who wish to remain with the merely visionary world make differing statements about the same subject at different times. On one occasion they tell us one thing, and on another something else. It is most unfortunate that visionaries usually have such a bad memory and generally forget what they told us the first time. They are unaware of what they have already told us.

In short, there is an immeasurable variety of manifestations. If with our present earthly 'I' we wanted to form correct judgements about everything presented to us in the visionary world, we should have to compare an infinite number of visions. But this would lead nowhere. We shall have to accept as a principle the fact that although the visionary realm is indeed a revelation of the spirit, it has not the slightest value as information. However many visions come to us, they are manifestations of the spiritual world, but they are not truths. If they are to become truths, we must first compare the various visions one person has, and indeed those that many others have as well, and that is impossible. Instead of this there is the possibility to develop further and reach the stage of Inspiration. When people attain the standpoint of Inspiration they will find that all the statements they make about something are alike. There are no more differences, nothing that appears differently to different persons. The experiences are the same for all those who have reached the same stage of development.

Now let us return to the other matter, the one that to some extent corresponds with this one, the matter that applies to the outer world. Here we compare the few seeds of life that reach their goal with the many that have sunk into the abyss. We know that they have to perish so that the outer world can continue to exist. But how do things stand with regard to the spiritual world and its visions and inspirations? We must be absolutely clear about the fact that once we have selected the visions, what we have before us are genuine spiritual realities, not merely pictures that give us information in the ordinary sense. I shall show you by a very important example why the latter is not the case. I shall explain how the selected visions stand in relation to the world just as we previously made clear how the life-seeds that have reached their goal stand in relation to the life-seeds in general that are used as food by others.

So what is the situation regarding the selected visions, those that live in the human being as real visions? I must draw your attention to something here. You must not believe that as a result of achieving clairvoyance a person then has the world of spirit living in him while the others do not. You must not imagine clairvoyance to mean that the soul of the clairvoyant contains expressions of spiritual reality while other souls do not. This would be wrong. Instead you must realize that the same things, the same spiritual incentives, live in a clairvoyant and in a non-clairvoyant. The clairvoyant differs from the non-clairvoyant only in that he sees them, whereas the other does not. The one bears them within him and sees them, the other also bears them within him but does not see them. It would be a great mistake to believe that a clairvoyant has in him something that others do not. Just as the existence of a rose does not depend on whether someone sees it or not, so is it with clairvoyance. Reality lives in the soul of the clairvoyant and in the soul of the non-clairvoyant although the latter does not see it. The only difference is that the one sees it and the other does not. The fact is that all the things the clairvoyant sees by means of his clairvoyance live in the souls of all human beings on earth. We should impress this firmly on our minds before we continue.

We shall now turn to observe what appears to be quite a different area, but this will later bring us back to what has already been said. Let us turn our attention to the animal world. The world of animals surrounds us in all kinds of individual shapes, those of lions, bears, wolves, lambs, sharks, whales and so on. We distinguish between these by forming external concepts of them, the concept lion, the concept wolf, lamb and so on. We must, however, not confuse the concept we form with what a lion or a wolf really is. You know that in spiritual science we speak of what we call group-souls. All lions share a common lion group-soul, all wolves a wolf group-soul. It is true that certain abstract philosophers maintain that what the animals have in common only exists in concepts, that 'wolfhood' does not exist in the real world. But this is incorrect. If you believe that 'wolfhood' as such, the group-soul objectively present in the spiritual world, does not exist except as a concept, you should consider the following.

In the world outside us there are creatures that we call wolves. Let us assume that the soul nature and characteristics of the wolf result from the kind of substance that forms the wolf's body. We know that the substance of an animal's body changes continually. The animal takes in new substance and discards the old. In this way its stock of substance changes all the time. The important thing is that there is something in the wolf that transforms the substances it absorbs into wolf-substance. Suppose all the refinements of science had enabled us to discover how long it takes for the wolf to renew its whole stock of substance. Then suppose we put the wolf in a cage for that duration and feed it only lambs, so that for the time it takes the wolf to renew its bodily substance entirely its food consists only of lamb-substance. If the wolf were nothing but the physical substance from which its body is made, it ought to have turned into a lamb by that time. Yet no one imagines that having been fed on lambs for such a long time the wolf will have changed into one. This shows that the concepts we form about the various animal shapes correspond to realities that are supersensible over against what exists in the sense-perceptible world.

The same goes for all the animals. The group-soul that is at the foundation of every species is what makes one animal a wolf and another a lamb, one a lion and another a tiger. We must form clear concepts of the group-souls. The concepts we usually form, especially of the animal world, tend to be rather incomplete, and this is due to the fact that in our present condition we do not enter very deeply into realities but tend to cling only to the surface of things. If we were to probe more deeply we would, when forming the concept wolf, find in our soul not only the abstract concept but also the mood of feeling that corresponds to this concept. A mood of feeling would form to accompany the concept, so that in forming the concept wolf we would experience what it is to be a wolf. We would feel the bloodthirsty nature of the wolf or the patience of the lamb.

That this does not happen today is due to the fact that after the luciferic influences[4] had been brought to bear the human being was prevented by the gods from also attaining 'life' in addition to 'knowledge'. (I can only put this symbolically, for otherwise it would go too far. You know the reality I mean.[5]) Man was not to eat from the tree of life. Consequently he has only knowledge and cannot recreate in himself an experience of the reality of life. This he can only do when he penetrates into this realm in a spiritual way. Then he has more than the abstract concept, for then he *lives* in what is expressed by the words 'the bloodthirstiness of the wolf', 'the patience of the lamb'.

You will now understand how great the difference is between these two situations. All these things are in conflict within us when the concepts are filled with the inmost essence of soul substance. A spiritual seeker and clairvoyant, however, must form these concepts for himself, he must rise to the level of these concepts. Once a clairvoyant has risen to this level it can be said that something of these things is now alive in him. In fact a living picture of the whole external animal world is alive in him then. We might be tempted to comment that the non-clairvoyant is rather fortunate in this respect, but I have already pointed out that actually there is no difference between clairvoyant and non-clairvoyant in this respect. What is in one is also in the other. The only difference is that the one sees it and the other does not. In reality the whole world of which I have been speaking is in every soul, only an ordinary person does not see it. It is this that surges up from the foundations of our soul, making us uneasy and dragging us down into doubt, pulling us hither and thither and creating the play of desires and instincts in us. What does not rise above a specific threshold, what expresses itself only in weaknesses, is none the less present. Those whose mental disposition is like this are linked with the world in a way that makes these feelings take possession of them, gripping them in their struggles and in life, bringing them into risky relationships with human and other beings. This is how things are—but why?

If this were not so, then the evolution of our earth would

have come to an end to some extent at the animal stage. The animal kingdom as it now is would have become a kind of ending. It would be unable to progress any further. All the group-souls of the animals living around us would be unable to develop onwards into the subsequent embodiments of our earth.[6] This would be a peculiar situation, for these group-souls of the animals would be in a position resembling—forgive the comparison, but it will show you what I mean—a community of Amazons into which no male may enter. Without men, such a community would die out. It would not die out spiritually, for the souls would pass on into other kingdoms, but as an Amazon community that would be its fate. In the same way the community of animal group-souls would die out if nothing else existed. What lives in the animal group-souls must be fertilized. It will be unable to cross the barrier in earthly evolution and pass on to the next embodiment of the earth in the Jupiter existence if it is not fertilized by what I have been describing. The animals perish in their earthly forms, but the animal group-souls are fertilized and appear on Jupiter having been prepared for a higher existence; they attain the next stage of their evolution.

What do human beings bring about by inwardly recreating the likeness of the living forms of those group-souls? By doing this they cultivate the fertilizing seeds for the group-souls which would otherwise be unable to evolve any further. Stimulated from outside to look at the animal kingdom, the human being develops within himself certain inner incentives that are fertilizing seeds for the animal group-soul. These incentives that arise as fertilizing seeds for the animal group-soul come into being through stimulus from outside. The visions of the clairvoyant do not come into being as the result of external stimulus, nor does the vision that is selected as the real one. It is simply there in the spiritual world and lives in the souls of human beings. You must not believe that nothing happens in the spiritual world when out of a multitude of grains of wheat many are eaten while only a few can develop to become new ears of wheat. While the grains are being eaten the spiritual part that is connected with them passes over into the human being. It is easiest for a clairvoyant to see what happens if he looks at the ocean containing many fish spawn of which only a few develop into fully grown fish. Those that develop into fully grown fish have little flames in them. But those that do not develop physically, those that descend into the abyss physically, engender mighty flaming light-forms. In them the spiritual part is all the more con-siderable. The same applies to the grains of wheat and other corns that are eaten. The material part is eaten; as they are being ground up, these grains of wheat that do not reach their goal engender a spiritual force that fills all our surroundings. This is what the clairvoyant sees when watching someone eating rice or anything similar. As the person absorbs the material part, uniting it with himself, the spiritual forces that were connected with the grains flash out in great streams. These things are not so simple for the spiritual observer, especially when the food eaten is not of plant origin. But I shall not say more on this today, since it is not for spiritual science to canvass on behalf of any particular party view, including that of vegetarianism.

The spiritual beings band together. Everything that appears to perish gives up its spirituality to the surroundings. This spirituality that is given up to the surroundings bands together with what lives within the human being in his visionary world, whether he is clairvoyant or not. And the visions selected in accordance with Inspiration are what fertilize the spirituality which is pressed out of the life-seeds that do not reach their goal, thus helping it to evolve further.

Through what it develops inwardly in this way, our inner being remains permanently related to the external world, working together with it. This external world would be doomed to perish and would be incapable of further evolution if we were unable to bring to it those fertilizing seeds. There is a spirituality out there in the world, but it is only half a spirituality. If this external spirituality is to have offspring, then that other spirituality living in our own inner being must join with it. What lives in us is no mere copy of what is outside, existing only in our thoughts; what lives in us belongs to what is outside us. It joins with what is outside us and continues to develop. Just as north pole and south pole must unite as magnetism or electricity if something is to happen, so must that which crystallizes out in our inner being in the world of visions unite with what flashes forth out of all that is seemingly perishing. Here are wonderful mysteries, gradually solved to show us how inner is linked with outer.

Let us now have a look at what surrounds us in the outer world and at the selected visions we have that are singled out from the immeasurable possibilities of visions. The visions we select as relevant to us serve our own inner development. Those from among the immeasurable field of visionary life that sink down do not sink down into nothingness but merge with the outer world, fertilizing it. The visions we have selected serve our own further development. The others depart from us and in our surroundings unite with all the life that has not achieved its goal.

Living creatures must assimilate as food that which has not reached its full life potential; we on the other hand must assimilate what we do not hand over to the outer world for its fertilization. There is purpose in this. Everything that is continually coming into being spiritually in the world would have to perish if we did not discard our visions and did not select only those that are revealed through Inspiration to be relevant.

Now we come to the second point of danger in visionary life. What is a person doing who simply takes all the immeasurable myriads of visions as truth without selecting what is relevant for him and extinguishing by far the greater number? What is such a person doing? Spiritually he is doing the equivalent of someone confronted with a field of wheat who does not use the greater part as food but allows every grain to be sown anew. This physical example gives a good idea of what is meant. Before long there would be no more room on the face of the earth for all that wheat. This could not go on, for everything else would die out for lack of food. The same happens to someone who takes everything as the truth, keeping it all inside himself and not extinguishing anything. Inside him it is as though he were to collect up all the grains of wheat and sow each one anew. Just as the world would soon be overwhelmed by wheat-fields and grains of wheat, so would such a person be overwhelmed with visions if he failed to select the relevant ones.

I have described the world that surrounds us, physically as well as spiritually, the animals and also the concepts we make about these things. I have shown that human beings must assign some purpose to their visions, and how the visionary world must unite with the outer world so that evolution can progress. Now take the human being as such. He is confronted by a group-soul, observes it, and says: 'Wolf.' This means that he has formed the concept 'wolf', and as he says the word the image springs up within him which for a non-clairvoyant, however, lacks inner soul and feeling substance; it is only an abstract concept. That which lives in the inner soul and feeling substance unites with the group-soul and fertilizes it when the human being pronounces the name 'wolf'. Were he not to pronounce the name, the animal kingdom as such would die out; and the same goes for the plant kingdom.

What I have just described with regard to man holds good for man alone, not for animals and also not for angels and so on. These have quite other tasks. Man alone exists in order that with his own being he may confront the outer world so that fertilizing seeds can arise that find expression in 'names'. Into man's inner being there has thus been laid what makes it possible for the animal and plant kingdoms to evolve further.

Let us now return to the starting-point we chose yesterday. Yahveh or Jehovah was asked by the ministering angels why it was man in particular that he wanted to create. The angels could not understand why. Then Jehovah called the animals and plants together and asked the angels what their names were. They did not know. They have tasks other than that of fertilizing the group-souls. Man, however, was able to tell the names. Thus Jehovah showed that he needed man, for otherwise creation would die out. In man those things evolve further that in creation have reached their goal and need a fresh stimulus in order that evolution can continue. Man had to be added to creation so that the fertilizing seeds could come into being that are expressed in the 'name'.

So we see that we have not been placed into creation without a purpose in life. Omit man from the scene, and the interim kingdoms would be unable to evolve any further. They would meet the fate that befalls a plant world when it is not fertilized. Only through the fact that man is brought into earth existence is the bridge built between the world that was there before and the world that comes afterwards. And man takes for himself, for his evolution, what lives as 'name' amid the immeasurable numbers of beings, thus bringing it about that he, too, can ascend alongside the whole of evolution.

Here, but not in a simple, abstract way, we have the answer to the question: 'What is the meaning of life?' Actually, this encompasses the abstract answer as well. Man has become a helper for the spiritual beings. He has become this through his whole nature. What he has in him has become the fertilizing seed for the whole of creation. He must exist, for without him creation could not exist. Knowing himself to be in the midst of creation, man thus feels that he is a participant in divine spiritual creativity.

So now we know why our inner life is as it is, why outside us there is the world of stars, clouds, the kingdoms of nature and all that belongs spiritually to these, and why inside us there is a world of soul life. We see that these two worlds belong together and that evolution only proceeds because they mutually affect one another. Outside us in space there spreads the immeasurable world. Inside us is our world of soul. We do not notice how what lives within us flashes out and unites with what lives outside us. We are unaware of being the arena in which this union takes place. What is inside us is the one pole, what is outside us in the world is the other pole. These two must unite in order that the evolution of the world may proceed. Our meaning, the meaning of man, is that we are permitted to participate in this.

With our ordinary knowledge in normal consciousness we know little of these things. But as we continue to make progress in what we know about them we become increasingly aware that the arena where the exchange takes place between the polar opposite forces—the north pole and south pole of the world, as it were—the place where they unite with one another, so that universal evolution can continue, is inside ourselves. We learn from spiritual science that the arena for the balancing of the world's forces is in us. We feel how the divine spiritual world lives in us as though in a central point, and how it unites with the outer world, and how the two thus mutually fertilize one another.

When we thus gain a feeling of being the arena and know that we play a part in all this, then we find our right place in life and grasp the whole meaning of life. We recognize that through persevering with spiritual science we become ever more aware of what initially lives unconsciously in us. Every development of higher spiritual powers rests on this. With our normal consciousness we do not know that something in us unites with something outside, but higher consciousness is permitted to observe this. Hence it is necessary for a degree of maturity to be reached, so that we do not indiscriminately mix what is within with what is without. What lives in us becomes a reality once we ascend to a higher consciousness; it is appearance only as long as we live in our ordinary, normal consciousness.

We shall participate in divine spiritual activity. But why shall we thus participate? Is there any meaning in it all if we are merely a kind of balancing apparatus for the polar opposite forces? Could not these forces balance each other just as well without us? A very simple consideration will show us how the matter stands. Here is a mass of force [draws on board]; one part lives inside and the other outside. It is nothing to do with us that these two parts confront one another; initially we keep them apart. But their coming together does depend on us. We bring them together within ourselves. This is a thought that stirs up the very deepest mysteries within us if we think it in the right way. The gods confront us with the world as a duality: objective reality is outside, soul life is in us. We are present; we are the ones who close the circuit, so to speak, thus bringing the two poles together. This takes place in us, it takes place in the arena of our consciousness.

This is where our freedom comes into play. It is in this that we become independent beings. The whole structure of the universe is not merely an arena, it is a domain of collaboration. The idea this raises is not so easily understood by the ordinary world, not even when it is framed in philosophical terms, for I tried this years ago in my small book *Truth and Knowledge*.[7] In it I showed how initially there is the activity of the senses, after which comes the inner world. I also showed that union, collaboration between them is necessary. This is that idea framed in philosophical terms. At the time I refrained from trying to show the whole spiritual mystery behind this, but even purely philosophically people did not understand what I meant.

We can now see what we should consider to be the meaning of our life. It has meaning because we become joint actors in the universal process. The world is divided into two opposing camps, and we are placed in the midst in order to bring them together. We should not imagine that this task is confined within narrow limits. I know an amusing gentleman in Germany who often writes in German journals.[8] In a newspaper article the other day he stated that as far as world evolution was concerned human beings ought forever to remain unable to solve the familiar world mysteries and that it would not be right for human beings to get to the bottom of them and solve them intellectually, for if they were to solve the mysteries intellectually there would be nothing left for them to do. Well, so doubts must forever remain regarding an intellectual understanding of world mysteries and imperfect things must always go on happening! This fellow has no idea of the fact that having reached its limit ordinary consciousness progresses of its own accord, so that a new polarity then appears that represents a new task in which the poles again have to be united. How long will poles have to go on being united? Until man has achieved a repetition of the divine consciousness within his own consciousness.

Having gained some inkling of this riddle's immense dimensions, we may now move forward to an abstract answer, for we now realize that in us there are fertilizing seeds for a spiritual world that cannot progress without us. We can once again enquire after the meaning of life, for now we have a broad base on which to work.

This is what we must now say: 'In the beginning of evolution there was the divine consciousness.' There it was— immeasurable. With it we are at the beginning of evolution. This divine consciousness first forms copies. How do these copies differ from the divine consciousness? They differ in that they were many, whereas the divine consciousness is one; they also differ in that they were void, whereas the divine consciousness was completely filled. So initially the copies are present as a multiplicity, but they are also empty, just as we had the empty 'I' as opposed to the divine 'I' that was filled with a whole world. This empty 'I' becomes the arena where the divine content, divided into two opposing camps, is continually being united. As the empty consciousness continually creates balances, it fills up more and more with what was originally in the divine consciousness. So evolution proceeds in that the individual consciousness becomes filled with that which the divine consciousness originally had as its content. This is brought about by a continual balancing within individualities.

Does the divine consciousness need this for its evolution? Many who cannot quite grasp the meaning of life ask this question. Does the divine consciousness need this for its own perfection, for its own evolution? No, it does not need this, for it possesses everything within itself. But the divine consciousness is not egoistic. It wishes to grant the content it has to an immeasurable number of beings. For this to happen these beings must first acquire it all, so that they have the divine consciousness within them and so that the divine consciousness shall be multiplied. Then what once existed as a unity at the beginning of world evolution will appear in vast numbers, but in due course these will once again fall away as the individual consciousnesses proceed to becoming entirely filled with the divine.

The evolution described here has always been thus for human beings. It was there during the Saturn existence, and similarly during the Sun and Moon existences.[9] In our Earth existence it is now clearly developed. In the Saturn existence the first rudiments of the physical body experienced this evolution, at the same time fertilizing towards the outside. In the Sun existence this involved the rudiments of the ether body, and so on. The process is the same, only it grows ever more and more spiritual. Less and less remains on the outside waiting to be fertilized. As human beings evolve further, more and more will live within them while less and less will be left outside still waiting to be fertilized. So in the end they will increasingly have within them what is now outside. The outer world will become their inner being. Becoming 'inward' is the other side of onward evolution.

To unite what is inside with what is outside, and to make inward what is external—these are the two items in accordance with which human beings progress in evolution. They will more and more come to resemble the divine, and finally they will become more and more inward. When the Vulcan existence comes everything will have been fertilized. Everything external will have become internal. To become divine is to become inward. To become inward is to become divine. That is the goal and meaning of life.

We cannot get at the truth of the matter, however, by

merely staking out some abstract concepts; we must go thoroughly into all the details. One must immerse oneself in all of it and go so thoroughly into detail that when one forms the name of animal or plant something arises within one's inner being that unites what lives in the word with what lies at the foundation of that animal or plant seed and then lives on in the spiritual world. Our view of the world calls for some improvement with regard to evolution, for what has Darwinism achieved in that respect? It speaks of the struggle for existence but fails to take into account that what is conquered in that struggle and therefore perishes is also subject to further evolution. A Darwinist sees only creatures that achieve their goal and others that perish. Spirit, however, flashes up from those that perish, so that there is evolution not only for the ones that win in the physical struggle. Those that seemingly perish go through an evolution in the spirit. This is the important thing.

This is how we can work towards finding the meaning of life. Nothing perishes, neither what is vanquished nor what is eaten up, for it is all fertilized spiritually and springs up spiritually once more. Much has disappeared throughout the evolution of earth and humanity without anyone being able to do anything about it. Think of the whole of pre-Christian evolution. We know what this pre-Christian evolution was like. In the beginning man came forth out of the spiritual world. Gradually he descended into the physical, sense-perceptible world. All that he possessed in the beginning, all that lived in him has vanished, just as the life-seeds that did not achieve their goal have vanished. We see countless things from the original stock of human evolution sink down into an abyss. While countless things sink down in the external evolution of human culture and life, up above the Christ-impulse is developing. Just as in the human being the fertilizing seed develops for the world around him, so does the Christ-impulse develop for the sake of all that seemingly perishes in the human being. Then the Mystery of Golgotha takes place. This is the fertilizing from above of all that has perished. A veritable change takes place in what has seemingly fallen away from the divine and sunk into the abyss. The Christ-impulse enters in and fertilizes it. From the Mystery of Golgotha onwards we see a new flowering and a new continuation in the course of earth evolution, brought about through the fertilization received with the Christ-impulse.

What we have learnt about polarity thus also proves to be true even for the greatest event in earthly evolution. In our time the seeds of culture lost in the ancient culture of Egypt are coming to life.[10] They are there in Earth evolution. The Christ-impulse has descended into them and fertilized them, and through being fertilized in this way a repetition of the Egypto-Chaldean culture has sprung up in our time. In the culture that will follow ours the ancient Persian epoch will come again, fertilized by the Christ-seed. In the seventh culture the ancient Indian epoch, that high spiritual culture emanating from the holy Rishis, will reappear in a new form, fertilized by the Christ-seed.

In this continuous development we see that what we have learned with regard to the human being can become a reciprocity: inner and outer, spiritual and physical which fertilize one another. Up above is the Christ-impulse and down below the fertilizing with the Christ-seed. Down below is earthly culture as it progresses; from above the Christ-impulse descends through the Mystery of Golgotha.

We now also see what it means to experience the Christ. The earth has to experience the cosmic mysteries, and the individual human being has to experience the divine mysteries. Through this the polarity was planted in man as in the earth.

The earth and that which is above it—that which united with the earth through the Mystery of Golgotha—have evolved like two opposing poles. Christ and earth belong together. Initially they had to evolve separately, so that it would become possible for them to unite. So we see that for things to come to true fruition it is necessary for them first to differentiate into polarities, polarities that can then unite again in order that life may progress. That is the meaning of life.

When we see things in this light we truly feel ourselves to be in the midst of the world, and that without us the world would signify absolutely nothing. Angelus Silesius, that profound mystic, made a remarkable statement which people might well find disconcerting at first: 'I know that without me God could not live an instant; were I brought to nought, he must needs give up the ghost.'[11] Confessional Christians who fulminate about a statement like this fail to take even the historical facts into account. Angelus Silesius was a profoundly pious man even before he became a Catholic in order to stand on what, in his opinion, was the firm ground of Christianity. Yet he pronounced this dictum. If you know Angelus Silesius you will not agree that coming from him it is an ungodly pronouncement. All things in the world stand opposed to other things, like polarities that could never meet if man were to disappear from the scene. The human being has his place in the midst and belongs there. When the human being thinks, the world thinks in him. Man is the arena; in this arena he brings the thoughts together. It is the same when he feels or exercises his will.

We can now understand what it means to direct our glance into the widths of space and say: 'The divine fills the human being, the divine that must unite with the earth-seed.' The human being can say: 'The meaning of life is within me.' The gods have set themselves goals, and they have chosen the arena in which these goals are to be achieved. The human soul is that arena. Therefore if the human soul looks deeply enough into itself and does not only want to solve the riddles of faraway space, then it will find there something in which the gods carry out their deeds; and the human being is playing his part. This is what I tried to express in words contained in my final mystery drama *The Soul's Probation*. I tried to express how the gods work in the inner being of man, how the meaning of the world finds expression in the soul of man and how the world will live on in the soul of man. What is the meaning of life? It is that this meaning will live in man himself. This is what I sought to express in words that the soul can say to itself:[12]

> Within your thinking cosmic thoughts hold sway,
> Within your feeling cosmic forces weave,
> Within your willing cosmic beings work.
> Lose yourself in cosmic thoughts.
> Experience yourself through cosmic forces.
> Create yourself from beings of will.
> In worlds' far reaches do not end
> through thinking's play of dreams.
> Begin within expanded spirit spheres
> and end in depths of your own soul:
> You'll find the aims of gods
> when you can know your self in you.

If we wish to say something that is true rather than something that merely occurs to us, it must always be founded in the secrets of the spirit. This is extremely important. Therefore you must not think that words used in occult works, whether in prose or poetry, can be in the same style as in ordinary works of literature. Works that genuinely stem from truth, from the world and its mysteries, come into being when the soul allows the cosmic thoughts to speak in it, when it allows itself to be truly fired by the cosmic feelings and not by any of its own personal feelings, and when it has truly created itself out of beings of will.

It is part of the mission of our spiritual movement that one should learn to distinguish between what streams out from world secrets and what our own fantasy invents arbitrarily. Our culture will evolve more and more to allow the place of arbitrary inventiveness to be taken by what lives in the human soul as the polarity to something spiritual to which it corresponds. Things created in this way become in their turn fertilizing seeds that unite with the spirit. They have a purpose in the world process. We gain quite a different sense of responsibility towards our actions if we know that what we bring into being are fertile seeds and not sterile ones that simply go up in smoke. We must allow these seeds to come into being out of the depths of the world-soul.

You might ask how this can be achieved. The answer is, by patience. By gradually more and more putting an end to any kind of personal ambition within oneself. We are more and more seduced by personal ambition to produce only what is personal instead of allowing the divine in us to speak. How are we to know that the divine is speaking in us? We must put an end to everything that comes only out of ourselves, and above all we must put an end to any kind of ambitious aspiration. Then the right polarity will be engendered in us, so that truly life-giving seeds are produced in our soul. (Impatience is the worst guide in life. It is what ruins the world.) If we succeed in this, you will see, as I have been explaining, that the meaning of life is attained in the manner described, through the fertilization of the outer with the inner. We then also see that if our inner life is not right we sow wrong fertilizing seeds in the world. What is the consequence? The consequence is that freaks are born into the world. There is a plethora of such freaks in our present culture. All over the world, for example, prose and poetry is written, you could almost say by steam-power, and soon hot-air balloons are likely to do the job as well. As early as the eighteenth century a well-known author wrote:[13] 'Nowadays a single country produces five times as many books as the earth requires for its good.' The situation has become much worse since then. These are things that surround present-day culture with spiritual beings incapable of living, beings that ought not to come into existence and that would not come into existence if people had the necessary patience. Patience will be born in the human soul eventually, like a kind of opposite pole, so that the soul does not madly scatter abroad what is merely a product of ambition and egoism.

This must not be taken as a kind of moral sermon, but as a statement of fact. It is a fact that the proceeds of ambition give rise in our soul to fertilizing seeds which bring freaks to birth in the spiritual world. To suppress these, or gradually to transform them, will be a fruitful task in a distant future. It is a mission of spiritual science to accomplish this task. It is the meaning of life that the world view of spiritual science shall thereby contribute to the whole meaning of life, that we shall be met by meaning everywhere in life, and that everywhere in life things shall be meaningful. What spiritual science wants to teach us human beings is that we are in the midst of meaning-fulness and can express it truly thus:

> Within your thinking cosmic thoughts hold sway,
> Within your feeling cosmic forces weave,
> Within your willing cosmic beings work.
> Lose yourself in cosmic thoughts.

Experience yourself through cosmic forces.
Create yourself from beings of will.
In worlds' far reaches do not end
through thinking's play of dreams.
Begin within expanded spirit spheres
and end in depths of your own soul:
You'll find the aims of gods
when you can know your self in you.

This, dear friends, is the meaning of life as human beings need to understand it at present.

This is what I wished to consider with you. If we understand it fully and make it entirely our own, then will the souls that have become divine make it effective in your soul.

You must ascribe the difficulty of understanding these lectures to the constraint that karma has imposed by allowing us only two short lectures for the explanation of something as important as the meaning of life. Much has only been hinted at and will have to come to life fully in your own soul.

Another polarity for you to consider is that a suggestion can be given which is to be worked on further in meditative contemplation; this further work gives meaning and content to all our collaboration, so that our souls begin to interplay with one another. This is the essence of genuine love. This, too, is a balancing of polarities. Where anthroposophical thoughts find entrance into souls they should there stimulate the other poles and find a balance with that other pole. This can work like a kind of anthroposophical music of the spheres. If we can thus work harmoniously in the spiritual world we shall, if we are true to anthroposophy, be united in this anthroposophical life.[14]

This is how I should like you to interpret today's gathering. These spiritual matters have been an expression of the spirit of love and they are dedicated to the spirit of love amongst us as anthroposophists. Through the spark that is ours this love will contribute to our mutual exchange of spiritual content. Then this love will become something that increasingly helps us not only to receive but also actively to strive in anthroposophy, so that spiritual science will become a means of spreading love that touches the inmost depths of the human soul. Such love will live on. Then, as human beings who have to be separated in space, we shall attain within our Society the endurance of this love from the times when karma has brought us together onwards to times when we have to be separated on the physical plane. We shall thus remain united, and having risen together to heights of divine spirit with our best spiritual faculties, we shall regard this as the true reason for remaining always together with the best that we possess in our souls. In this way, my dear friends, let us remain united with one another.

PART TWO:

ILLNESS AND HEALTH

3. Illusory Illness[1]

Throughout their lives human beings find themselves placed between two forces. On the one hand there is the sequence of events, the flow of external facts exerting all kinds of influences, while on the other each individual possesses his or her own inner strength. Even a cursory glance at life is sufficient to show that we must find a necessary balance between the forces and facts bombarding us from all sides and the life unfolding within us. Having received one impression after another throughout the day, we long for an opportunity to be alone and compose ourselves, sensing that health is only to be found through achieving a proper balance.

Goethe expressed this in beautiful lines that encompass the depth and breadth of life and penetrate to the very riddles of existence:[2]

> For every force sweeps outward into space
> To live and work here, there and everywhere;
> While on the other hand the teeming world
> From every side confines and takes away.
> Between the inner storm and outer conflict
> The spirit hears a word slow comprehended:
> From powers that fetter every living being
> *That* man is free who overcomes himself.

The last two lines contain much wisdom about life: 'From powers that fetter every living being *that* man is free who overcomes himself.' As it storms ahead in its potential for continual unfolding and development our inner being comes up against all that approaches us from outside. We find a balance between inner and outer when we overcome ourselves. This will be the leitmotif for our considerations today and the day after tomorrow. The two themes belong together. We shall look at illusory illness today and in two days' time at the feverish pursuit of health, which is its inevitable complement.

You will see the justification for these words as our considerations proceed, for they will lead us to some of the cultural trends of our time and show us the task that spiritual science must fulfil in order to counteract them.

The first thing that comes to mind in connection with the words 'illusory illness' is the phenomenon we meet quite often of a person experiencing genuine pain and listlessness in consequence of some imagined illness. This is one of the very realms in which spiritual science should exercise its cultural task. Important things depend on this, but before we look in detail at what spiritual science has to say about it, let us examine a few present-day observations, all taken from real life.

On one of my journeys (by train from Rostock to Berlin) I shared a compartment with a lady and a man who soon began chatting with one another. The man's behaviour was quite peculiar, for after only a few words he stretched out full length on the seat saying that he could only bear life lying down. The lady said she was from the eastern part of the country and had been to a Baltic spa. Having been overcome by homesickness the day before, she had decided to go home, she said, and promptly burst into tears. Encouraged by the lady's tears, the man began telling tales about his state of health. Suffering from many illnesses he journeyed from one sanatorium to the next without getting well again. On hearing this the lady said that she understood a great deal about illness and claimed that many people in her home district owed her their health and

their life. Then the man described one of his numerous illnesses, whereupon the lady dipped into her heart's fountain of
knowledge and advised him on a cure, which the man wrote
down. After a few minutes the second illness was recounted,
and this went on until, much to his delight, the man had
written down 13 cures. His only worry then was whether he
would be able to get the necessary medicaments immediately,
since the train was not due to arrive in Berlin until nine in the
evening. The lady reassured him about this.

Strangely enough, it never occurred to the man that the
lady herself was ill. She continued to talk, saying that she had
much sympathy, and proceeded to recount her own illnesses,
telling of all the many places in which she had sought cures.
The man recommended a work by Lahmann.[3] After her
description of another illness he recommended a second
leaflet, and this continued until the lady had made a note of
five or six works which she intended to purchase next day.
Finally she wrote down Lahmann's address. Meanwhile the
train had arrived in Berlin. Each had written down the other's
recommendations and, well pleased, they went their separate
ways.

Anyone observing these two with a modicum of insight
would have noticed that while the lady was genuinely suffering from a number of maladies, the man merely lacked the will
to be well. Had he been able to muster the will to be well he
would have been perfectly healthy. This is symptomatic of
something we frequently encounter today, and if we look
closely we will see how it ties in with our next observation.

When walking in the mountains we often notice ancient
forts, ruined castles and so on that remind us of the olden days
when people strove for strength of spirit or when external
might dominated. Such forts have fallen into ruin today, but
in the vicinity of these monuments to strength we frequently

THE WILL TO BE WELL.

see sanatoriums one beside the other. I made the following observation recently, in a district with a particularly large number of these institutions, when I had to call in at one of them for a quarter of an hour or so when the patients were just going in to lunch. I formed the conviction that there was not one among the hundreds present who seriously needed the regime of a sanatorium.

Let us now move on to more intimate observations that are to be found in the accounts of thoughtful physicians today, for fortunately there are indeed some who concern themselves with the soul as well as the body. I choose an example by a physician who would most probably regard everything anthroposophical as nonsense, an individual who would surely be quite uninfluenced by anything spiritual science might say. This prominent physician has recorded various cases of individuals resembling the couple I met in the train, who merely provide a particularly absurd example.[4]

The physician was called to attend a girl who was displaying all the symptoms of meningitis. Being a man of good clinical sense, he asked the usual questions that are asked in such cases, but none of them elicited pertinent answers. Finally, when he was alone with her, it emerged that the young lady was about to leave school but that in the coming year there were to be particularly interesting lectures that she wanted to attend. She had fallen ill because the rest of her family opposed her wish to remain at school. The physician said, 'I shall intervene on your behalf, but you must get out of bed immediately and join the family at table.' The young lady did so. A few minutes later she joined her family at table and was no longer ill.

Take another example. A physician, very skilful and well known, for whom I have always had a considerable regard, was operating on a patient's knee. The patient's brother was present at the operation and when he heard a cracking sound this brother experienced excruciating pain. The operation was successful, but the brother fell ill and failed to get better for a whole year.

This shows how strongly fantasy and perverted imagination can influence the soul and how imitations of diseases can stem from the soul and manifest like genuine diseases. But one must not exaggerate this presumption. The physician just mentioned was very skilful and did not allow himself to assume that it applied in every case. He was consulted by a lady who had had unbearable pain in her knee ever since the death of her husband. The many other physicians who had already treated her had done so in the assumption that the origin of her illness was psychological and resulted from what she had gone through when her husband died. This physician was clear-sighted enough to see that the cause in this case was not psychological. He found a large corn on the lady's heel, and having operated on it sent her to Bad Gastein in order not to embarrass his colleagues.

We have now illumined our subject by a number of observations that show how strongly the imagination, the psychological image, can affect the physical organism. You might be tempted to regard what we are talking about as illusions of illness rather than genuine ones. But once you have realized that everything in the physical body is an expression of the spirit, that everything with which our senses are confronted is a manifestation of something supersensible, you will no longer take these things so lightly. Even in seemingly quite remote instances we find that it is often a question of the soul influencing the body. So once real pain sets in, the illusion—something we initially regard as rather trivial or risible—can indeed lead to the beginnings or even the further stages of genuine illness. Such illusions cannot be shrugged off so lightly. In order to go into this more deeply we shall have to open our soul to something we have frequently spoken about here—the nature and being of man.

To spiritual science, what the human being presents at first glance is only an outer aspect. Our physical body is only one aspect of our being, one that we have in common with all other creatures around us. Beyond it we have an ether body, which penetrates our physical body, as is the case with every living creature. The ether body combats the disintegration of the physical body. The third aspect of our being is the astral body, which is the bearer of pleasure and displeasure, joy and pain, passion and desire, the lowest urges as well as the highest ideals. We have this body in common only with the animal kingdom. The aspect that makes the human being the jewel in the crown of creation is the ego, the 'I', which sets him apart from every other creature. For our considerations here these four aspects together make up the total human being.

In this connection we must be clear that everything visible to our eyes derives from the spirit alone. Nothing material exists that is not founded in the spirit.

There is an analogy we have used before, that of the child who shows us some ice. We say, 'This is water in another form.' Whereupon the child says, 'You call this water, but it is ice,' to which we reply, 'You do not know the process by which water becomes ice.' This is how it is for someone who does not know that matter is a condensed form of spirit. For the student of spiritual science, however, everything that is visible in us stems from the same source as our astral body. Our ether body and our physical body are successive condensations of our astral body, as the picture of the ice shows. We have some water and cause part of it to turn into ice, so that we have ice in water. In a similar way the ether body and physical body have condensed out of the astral. The astral body is the part that is left in its original state.

When we are confronted by health or illness we can say that these are expressions of certain forces that may be observed in the astral body. This refers of course to illnesses that arise from within, not those caused by external factors such as a broken leg, an upset stomach or a cut finger. In speaking about illnesses that arise from the human being's inherent nature we can ask: 'Is the link between astral and physical body something that belongs only to the past? Is there not perhaps still a connection between the internal processes of our soul, pleasure or pain, and the physical condition of our body? Can we maintain that to some extent a person's external health depends on his harbouring various feelings or experiencing certain thoughts?' If we can fill ourselves with conceptions like these we shall be able to throw light on important knowledge that could be of value, especially nowadays.

People are no longer able to raise their sights to the fact that the physical body is not the only aspect of the human being. Rather than a matter of what we believe theoretically, this is much more a question of the inner attitude we carry in our soul regarding the human being's higher aspects. To get down to what is really involved, let us call to mind the dispute between Rudolf Wagner and Carl Vogt, author of a paper on blind faith and science.[5] Wagner represented the spiritualist standpoint, while Vogt saw the human being as nothing but a conglomeration of physical things, atoms. To him thoughts were nothing more than an excretion from the brain, a vapour arising from movements in the brain, and in death the substances ceased to exude this vapour of thoughts. Wagner disagreed, but in a way that brings to mind the way parents of, say, eight children can pass on their mental attitude to all eight in varying degrees. Like so many others, he also favoured an entirely material image of the spirit as a misty formation. What matters to us, though, is that one must raise one's sights to attitudes and feelings that genuinely comprehend the spirit. There are many people today who want nothing to do with materialism and yet have an entirely materialistic understanding of spirit. Even many anthroposophists think of the spirit as attenuated matter, for even anthroposophy covers up a good deal of shamefaced materialism.[6]

In those who are unable to raise their sights to the lofty realm of spirit an inner desolation, an emptiness, a lack of belief in anything beyond the material realm gradually makes itself apparent. When this takes hold of the feelings, when it eats into all belief, all feelings of the soul, when such people look out into the world and fail to sense in it anything beyond what they can see, then something comes to the fore that increasingly engenders in them the grossest bodily egoism through which their own body grows more and more important to them as their attitude of mind becomes further and further removed from what Goethe's words express:

From powers that fetter every living being
That man is free who overcomes himself.

This brings us to an important phenomenon connected with materialism which is likely to develop fully in the future if spiritual science fails to conquer it. If human beings only grasp intellectually what they perceive through their senses there will be consequences for their health that will differ entirely from those that will arise if they regard the world as it confronts them as a sense-perceptible expression of something spiritual. Materialistic thinking and spiritual-scientific thinking both have a profound effect on the inner human being. The difference between materialistic or spiritual-scientific thinking is more than a merely theoretical matter. The one works to desolate, the other to enrich inwardly. A simple example is to say that you are more likely to become short-sighted if you absorb impressions passively during your period of development, whereas if you confront impressions actively your eyesight will remain good. You need to develop creative powers from within. Anything that helps you to become a centre of creative, productive strength will have a health-giving effect. If you do not create from within, your creative power will go to waste and your whole being will be crushed by external impressions. All external impressions must be countered by strength from within. At the same time the reverse is also necessary. You also have to develop an inner activity that shuts itself off from the outside, that is not outwardly visible.

There are two experiences of soul in which you should immerse yourself, for they demonstrate that the human being possesses an inner fullness that rays outwards and that he searches for a middle point from which to direct his activities outwards. Studying these two types of feeling, these two directions, we can be led deep into the phenomenon of human illness. The one feeling, fear, is negative; the other, shame, is positive, although this is also something negative. Imagine yourself faced with an event that fills you with fear and dread. If you do not look at this from the materialistic point of view but include the astral body in what you see, you will understand that turning pale is an expression of energy currents in the human being. Why does the soul affect the distribution of blood in this way? It does so because it is trying to create a centre of will from which it can work outwards. Figuratively speaking, it gathers the blood to the centre in order to be able to work outwards from there. With shame the reverse is the case. We blush. Blood flows from the centre to the periphery. The feeling of shame points to a situation in which we want to extinguish what is visible, in which we want to extinguish our 'I'. We want to make our 'I' weaker and weaker so that it becomes invisible externally. We want a way of losing our self or of dissolving into the universe, into the world soul or, if you will, into the surroundings, in order not to be visible externally.

This polarity of shame and fear points to important conditions of the ether body and the astral body. They are two instances in which the forces of the astral body become visible externally. Fear and shame express themselves in bodily states, and on further reflection you will realize that in fact all soul processes can have effects in the processes of the organism. This is true, and spiritual science teaches us about it. There is a link between the two even though we may be unaware of it as yet.

Let us now turn to the fact that today's abstract thinking has the least imaginable effect on the organism. What we learn in our abstract sciences has the least imaginable effect on the body. The principle behind these sciences is that we must transform what we see and perceive into abstract concepts. These sciences do not want to admit that the human being has any kind of innate creative wisdom, or that the soul on its own can bring forth anything about the world. When we perceive something in an external manner, our soul of course creates nothing in response. In the deepest sense there is no inner creativity with which to counter external impressions. Scientists do not wish to discover things out of themselves.

The belief that the human being can find nothing within himself is so deeply rooted that it must be seen as the cause of the desolating effect knowledge has when it is attached solely to external facts.

What is the remedy that would counter this for humanity? If

inner wisdom and truth, inner creativity of spirit, were to accompany outer science, this would be the remedy. It is a remedy that is to be found in true spiritual science. It lays open the sources through which we can discover out of ourselves what lies behind outer things. Some people are oppressed by things, but those who see what cannot be absorbed by any outer perception, those who take in what they see in this way, they are creating the counterpart to outer perception that is necessary if soul and body are to be healed through and through. This healing of the soul cannot be achieved by means of abstract theories and thoughts; these are too meagre and inadequate. Powerful effects are achieved, however, when a concept is transformed into a picture.

What does this mean? The best way to understand it is to think of what is meant by evolution. We have been told that once upon a time the simplest living creatures developed ever more complicated forms until the human being appeared. This is, however, nothing but an abstract, meagre concept; the same can also be found in the evolutionary theories of many theosophies in which people begin from the Logos and then proceed in all kinds of abstract concepts such as differentiation, evolution, involution and so on. Such ideas are too weak to have any effect on the organism. Something that is strong in its effect, however, is what lives in our soul when we ponder on a picture or an Imagination that we have called up before our soul.[7] (We have been learning to do this since the fourteenth century.) Let me show you a picture of this kind.

A pupil was told: 'Examine a plant, place it side by side with the human being and compare the two. Do not compare the head with the flower and the feet with the roots.' (Not even Darwin, the reformer of science, did this.) The pupil was told: 'The roots correspond to the head, for the human being is an upside-down plant.' (This is something that spiritual science, too, has always maintained.) A part of the plant chastely allows the sun to kiss it so that a new plant can be born from it. In the human being this part is turned modestly in the opposite direction down towards the centre of the earth. The animal exists in the middle, between the two. It is a half turned around plant.

Summarizing what lives in plant, animal and man, Plato described the world soul as being crucified upon the cross of the world body.[8] The world soul that encompasses plant, animal and man is crucified on the body of the world. (This is how spiritual science has always explained the cross, too.)

Having been introduced to this significant picture the pupil was told: 'You see how the human being evolves from the dim consciousness of the plant via the animal upwards to the point where he finds self-awareness. The sleeping human being has an existence like that of the plant; by permeating the pure, chaste plant material with the body of passions he has risen higher than the plant, but also in a sense sunk lower. There would have been no other way for him to acquire his higher "I"-consciousness; but now he must once more transform his passionate nature. In the future the human being will have an organ of reproduction that will be without passion, chaste as the flower's calyx.' In this way the pupil was told of a time when the human being will bring forth his own kind without passion. This was depicted in the Grail schools through the picture of the Holy Grail.

So here we have evolution depicted not in thoughts but in a picture, an Imagination. It would be possible to transform into pictures all knowledge imparted to us via abstract concepts, and we would accomplish a good deal if we did so. By bringing this most meaningful ideal of evolution alive before our inner eyes and developing it further, up to the Imagination of the Holy Grail, we would gain nourishment for our power of judgement. Not only would it provide support for our intellectual understanding, but our whole life of feeling would twine around it as well. You tremble in awe before the great cosmic secret when you see the evolution of the world in all its truth and grasp it in pictures like these. In accordance with spiritual laws such pictures have a harmonizing effect on the organism. Abstract thoughts have no effect, but such pictures act as a health-giving inner stimulus. Pictures bring about strong feelings, and if they are true cosmic images, Imaginations, then their effect is health-giving.

Pictures

By transforming what they see externally into these pictures, human beings learn to extricate themselves from their inner realm, and the storm is resolved into harmony. They overcome those 'powers that fetter every living being' and assume kinship with everything that comes to meet them. They flow out, and through their feelings grow into union with the world. Their inner self is expanded to become a spirit universe.

When, however, they are unable to form such Imaginations, then all their strength flows inwards and they remain stuck with their 'I'. This is the mysterious cause of a phenomenon we can observe in so many of our contemporaries. Having rejected the old forms of religion, people are now turning in on themselves, living increasingly inside their own inner being and becoming totally bound up in themselves. The less human beings have the opportunity to expand into general cosmic existence, the more they become conscious of what is going on in their own organism. This causes false feelings of anxiety and illusions of illness.

The picture works outwards from the soul into the organism, and a bodily disposition that is healthy is brought about by true pictures. False pictures also leave their imprint, however, giving rise to psychological disorders that subsequently lead to bodily disorders. This is the real cause of illusory illness. Those who close themselves off from the great cosmic relationships will be incapable of repelling what comes towards them. Conversely, those who have taken great pictures into themselves will be immune to deception by false ones. For example such a person would not imagine, as happens sometimes, that he detected the current from an induction coil passing through his body when no such current was present.

Every picture that has no place in the overall cosmic nexus, every picture that works merely as a one-sided image of daily life, is a picture that leads to illness. The only way we can correct what needs to be corrected is to look up from the individual, lone situation to the great mysteries of the cosmos. Something that works properly on the soul can be very powerful indeed, and we should not neglect things of this kind that have been created throughout our cultural history. Today we are discussing our instincts about health, and we can also consider dramatic tragedy from this angle. When people watched a tragedy in ancient Greece they shared in the sufferings, were borne along and gripped by them. By the time they left the amphitheatre they knew that the hero had won the day against those sufferings, and thus that human beings are capable of overcoming worldly suffering. By facing suffering and overcoming suffering the human being becomes healthy, whereas turning one's glance inwards makes for illness.

To see in an outward picture what lives within you makes you well. That is what Aristotle meant when he said that the hero in the tragedy goes through suffering and fear in order to cure human beings of suffering and fear.[9] Such things have far-reaching effects, and the student of spiritual science can tell you why ancient peoples presented human souls with pictures by means of fairy-tale and legend. People were shown pictures of aspects living in their soul from which they ought to turn away. The gory nature of fairy-tales is a health-giving educational means. If you can follow myths from this angle you will learn a lot from them. For example if people see revenge depicted outwardly in a picture, if they see something from which they should turn away, the effect will be that they do indeed succeed in overcoming it. The deepest wisdom lies hidden even in the most gory tales.

Our inner harmony is disturbed if we constantly gape into our own soul; it is made well when we look out into the all, into the cosmos. But you have to know what pictures to choose. Confronted with a melancholy person, a hypochondriac for example, who cannot get over something that has happened, you will fail if you try to cheer him up with jolly music. You will achieve the opposite of what you intend, even if for the moment this may not appear to be the case. In the depths of his soul such a person will find the music insipid and dreary, though he may not admit it. You will need grave pictures even if they appear to upset him at first.

So you see, a specific way of treating the soul can come about through spiritual science. You cannot counteract illusory illness by a single means for it is a product of our materialistic age with its lack of creativity. But by looking more deeply into things you can explain the false, groundless fears and all those feelings that express psychological imbalance—depression for example. In the same way you will also find the remedies. Someone who understands what is happening will not have trouble in detaching himself from his 'I'. When a situation arises there is usually an initial cause which then becomes exaggerated. For example a person knocks his knee on the edge of the table. Lacking greater thoughts that would take his whole attention he cannot extricate himself from the pain which therefore continues to get worse. The doctor is called and suggests a remedy. Thereupon the other knee starts to hurt as well, followed by an elbow, and so on. Finally the patient can no longer move either legs or arms, and all because he knocked his knee. There may be reasons why his attention becomes focused on a particular point, but other things exist that can redress the balance. As life today grows increasingly difficult people will only find a balance if they allow spiritual science to work upon them. If they do they will be armed against the negative influences of civilization.

There are, however, also external reasons for the lack of creative powers. The facts speak loudly. Look at the animals that are brought into captivity as part of our civilization. They fall ill, which never happens to them in the wild. This is caused by the strong influences from the environment that affect both man and animal. Because their evolution has reached its conclusion the animals have no inner force with which to counter these. As civilization progresses, human beings, too, will become decadent if they fail to counter external influences with their creative power. By inner activity they must reshape and transform these influences, and if they do so they may even use them for their further development.

An individual who generates a radical materialistic theory is healthy for he is creating outwards from within. But adherents of such a theory grow dull because they are not bringing forth any creative force of their own. There is no value in your reading books even on spiritual science if you do not inwardly recreate them. If you do, you are inwardly sharing in their creation, but if you do not, it is tantamount to not studying them in the first place. The important thing is to feel the strength that wants to press forward and take in the outer world so that we can find a balance between external impressions and inner creativity. The individual must free himself from the external strife in the world so that this does not impinge on him more and more until it stifles him. We must bring about the counter-thrust. The external impression must be met by the counter-thrust from within. Then we free ourselves of it, but otherwise it increasingly turns us in upon ourselves. If we persist in turning our attention inwards, a picture of suffering arises before our soul. But if we express the balance between the inner power urgently pressing forwards and the external power, then we merge with the external world.

Today we have got to know illusory illness in a deeper sense as a phenomenon of our time. Our starting-point was the wish of spiritual science to be the remedy that will help human beings free themselves from themselves and thus of all those 'powers that fetter'. Every power that fetters makes us ill. In this way we begin to understand the deeper core of Goethe's words:

> For every force sweeps outward into space
> To live and work here, there and everywhere;
> While on the other hand the teeming world
> From every side confines and takes away.
> Between the inner storm and outer conflict
> The spirit hears a word slow comprehended:
>> From powers that fetter every living being
>> *That* man is free who overcomes himself.

4. The Feverish Pursuit of Health[1]

Good health is something for which everyone longs, and it is surely true to say that this longing is not solely the product of egoistic feelings and wishes but also has to do with our justified desire to work. We owe our ability to work, to achieve something in the world, to our good health—and that is why we appreciate our health as a very special commodity. It is rather significant that good health should be desirable because it enables us to work, for this highlights the circumstances in which good health is desirable at all. It may sound strange to maintain that good health is only worth pursuing under certain circumstances, but our considerations today will show that good health is one of those commodities we are most likely to acquire if we seek it not for its own sake but for the sake of something else. We only need to look around us to see that this does not always happen.

To speak of a feverish pursuit of health, of a fevered urge to attain good health, may sound strange, but this is definitely a phenomenon we can observe nowadays. Most people press for good health in countless ways, and the rush for good health is going on everywhere. There are regions in which old forts and ruined castles abound, telling of olden times when monks and knights possessed strength of spirit and strength of body. These buildings have fallen into disrepair, but sanatoriums now abound in the same regions. In all history, when has there ever been a culture offering so many specialized ways of achieving health by means of natural diet, water cures or fresh air treatments? People gather at spas in droves to be cured by air and sun.

An acquaintance called on me early last summer on his way to a sanatorium. He had managed to scrape together four consecutive weeks of leave which he intended to spend there, for in his opinion there could be no better way of spending this time more or less satisfactorily than in a sanatorium. I did not have the heart to deprive him of his hopes by suggesting that his project might be futile. He called on me again on his return journey and showed me the diary he had kept of all the things he had been made to do with his body during those four weeks. Again I did not have the heart to disappoint him, but I could scarcely refrain from asking: 'Do tell me, when were you more driven? During your whole year at work or in these past four weeks being hurried from heat to cold, from dry to wet, and scrubbed up and down with all kinds of brushes?' The worst part of it was that after some weeks he told me this cure had done him as little good as all the others over the past 30 years (for he has tried something different every summer). If you like this man, all you can do is feel rather sorry for him in his feverish pursuit of health. What crowds of people nowadays rush to mesmerists and spiritual healers! What myriads of pamphlets there are on being 'in tune with the infinite' and similar subjects![2] In short, the feverish pursuit of health is flourishing in our time.

The question we might now ask is: 'Are these people actually ill? No doubt there is some small thing the matter with them, but is there any prospect of attaining health through all these cures?'

There is an old saying favoured by rather simple people, and although such people often retain much wisdom in their sayings, this particular one is wrong. They maintain that there are many illnesses but only one state of good health. This is foolish. There are as many states of good health as there are individuals, for every human being has his or her own particular state of good health. In other words all general standard prescriptions as to what is and what is not good for people are nonsense. Those who have fallen under the sway of the feverish pursuit of health are the very ones who suffer most from general prescriptions about health and—through believing that such a thing as a generally valid state of good health exists—also from the presumption that one specific remedy should be followed because it is the very one that will make them better. It is incredible how people fail to realize that you cannot generalize, that a sun bath may be good for one person and very bad for another. Though this is perhaps admitted in general, people do not act upon it in specific cases. We must be quite clear about the fact that good health is entirely relative and also that it changes all the time, especially as regards the human being, who is the most complex creature on the whole earth.

Even a brief look into spiritual science will help us penetrate deeply into human nature and recognize how variable so-called good health is. Although much importance is attached to evolution in connection with material things, people forget entirely for most of the time that the human being, too, is engaged in a process of evolution.

What do we mean by saying that the human being is engaged in a process of evolution? Let us recapitulate what has been said about the being of man. The physical body is only one part of our being, and it is held in common with all of nature, both animate and inanimate. As a second aspect we have the ether or life body which we possess in common with all living creatures. This body wages a continual battle against everything that is intent on destroying the physical body. If the ether body were to depart from it, the physical body would immediately become a corpse. The third aspect is the astral body, which we have in common with the animals—the bearer of joy and sorrow, of every feeling and inner picture, of happiness and pain (we also call it the consciousness body). The fourth aspect is the 'I', the centre of our being, which makes man the jewel in the crown of creation. The 'I' transforms the three bodies, working outwards from the centre.

Imagine a member of an unspoilt tribe of long ago side by side with an average individual today, and these two beside a highly educated idealist. The member of an unspoilt tribe is as yet ruled by his instincts and urges. Today's average person refines his urges, denying himself the satisfaction of some and perhaps replacing these with laws or high-minded religious ideals. In doing this he is re-working his astral body from the centre of his being, from his 'I'. In consequence his astral body develops two parts. One remains as it was in the member of an unspoilt tribe while the other is transmuted into the spirit-self or manas. Through the impressions gained from art or the great inspirations of the founders of religion the human being also works on his ether body creating the buddhi, the life-spirit. And through practising the exercises given by spiritual science one can even work towards transforming the physical body into atma, spirit-man. In this way human beings work unconsciously or consciously on their three bodies.

If we were able to look back into the far distant past of human evolution we would find unspoilt cultures, simple modes of living. The tools of those people and the way of life they needed for the satisfaction of their cultural and bodily needs would all be simple. Everything is evolving, and most importantly the human being is evolving.

Imagine as vividly as you can the member of an unspoilt tribe grinding grain to flour between two stones, and picture to yourself the other things all around him. Compare this with an individual of more recent civilizations and think what surrounds him, what he sees all around him from morning till night. He has to contend with the horrible racket of trams, buses and so on in big cities. In trying to understand how evolution progresses, we should apply our understanding of those more simple things to the cultural process as such.

Goethe said that the eye was formed by the light for the light.[3] If we had no eyes we should see neither light nor colours. So where do our eyes come from? What Goethe said was: 'The light drew forth eyes from undifferentiated organs.' Similarly the ears were formed by sound and our sense of temperature by heat. The human being has been formed by what is spread all around him in the whole wide world. Just as eyes owe their existence to light, so do other subtle structures in our organism owe their existence to what surrounds us. The simple, unspoilt world is the darkroom that still retains many as yet undeveloped organs. What light did for the undifferentiated organs out of which the eyes developed is what the environment did for that member of an unspoilt tribe of old. In the way we live today our environment works on us in quite a different manner. We cannot revert to those unspoilt cultures of old because an ever more intense and strong spiritual light has been at work around us, calling forth ever more new features.

We can gain a conception of this transforming cultural process by trying to imagine what it must be like for creatures who are also exposed to these influences but who are not capable of undergoing any further change. These are the animals. They are structured differently from human beings. Animals in the physical world have a physical body, an ether body and an astral body, but on the physical plane they have no 'I'. So on the physical plane animals are incapable of transforming their three bodies and therefore cannot adapt to an imposed new environment. The day before yesterday we mentioned wild animals in captivity. In their wild environment they would never suffer from tuberculosis, tooth decay and so on, but they do in captivity. In captivity or similar situations they manifest decadence in quite a number of ways.

As civilization and culture progress, human beings are continually subjected to new conditions. This is the nature of culture. Without it there would be no evolution and no human history. What we saw in the way the physical body of the animals was affected by the experiment with nature would be quite the opposite in the case of humans. Being in possession of an 'I', the human being can work inwardly on the impressions bearing down on him from external culture. He is inwardly active, adapting first his astral body to the changed conditions, restructuring it entirely. By developing in this way he enters ever more refined cultures and receives ever new impressions. Initially these express themselves as feelings and sensations. If human beings were passive in such situations, if they remained inactive and generated no creativity, then, like the animals, they would become stunted and ill. What distinguishes human beings is the fact that they can adapt and gradually transform ether body and physical body, beginning with the astral body. But to do this they must be inwardly strong enough, otherwise they fail to achieve a balance between what approaches them from the outside and the strength they can muster from within. We would be stifled by the impressions, just as the animals are stifled in their cages because they are incapable of generating any creativity. Human beings do possess this inner activity. They must constantly counter the spiritual light around them, as it were bringing forth eyes with which they can confront it.

Anything that results in disharmony between external impressions and inner life is unhealthy. In big cities we can clearly see what happens when external impressions grow ever more powerful. When we dash along faster and faster, when we have to let loud noises and rushing human beings hurry by without taking a stand against them, without generating any counter-activity—this is unhealthy. By 'taking a stand' I do not mean an intellectual reaction so much as a reaction of feeling; our soul, indeed the very life in our body has to take a stand.

Looking at a particular illness that has come up in our time and never used to exist will help us understand this more clearly. Take a person who is not accustomed to absorbing very much, someone who is rather poor in soul. When faced with all kinds of impressions such a person finds himself up against a completely incomprehensible outer situation. This often happens to women, but many men are also affected; their inner being is too weak, too unstructured to absorb it all. In consequence hysterical illnesses begin to manifest. All such illnesses can be attributed to the imbalance I have just described.

Another form of illness comes about when life makes us want to comprehend too much of what confronts us from our environment. It is mostly men who are afflicted by the 'reason why' disease. Such people get into the habit of constantly asking, 'Why, why?' Today we are too polite to react—as the founder of a denomination is said to have done when asked what God did prior to creating the world—with the rejoinder: 'He cut canes with which to whip those who ask silly questions.'[4] This questioning condition is the opposite of what afflicts someone who is hysterical. Here the restless longing to find answers to every enigma is too great. It is the expression of an inner mood. The constitution of a person who never tires of asking 'Why?' differs from that of other people. His inner processes of soul and body differ from those of someone who only asks 'Why?' when prompted by some outer circumstance. It is this that lies behind every state of hypochondria, from the lightest cases to the most serious illusory illnesses. It is an effect of today's culture and civilization. People need to be open to an extent that enables them to deal inwardly with whatever comes to meet them. We can thus explain why so many individuals get the urge to shed our civilization and even to have done with this life. It is because they are not up to coping with what is coming at them from all sides. They long to get away. Such individuals are too weak to muster enough inner strength with which to counter the external impressions.

Precisely because our life is so very varied we cannot speak today of a generally valid model of good health. This person is in one situation, that person in another. To a considerable extent what has come into being within each of us is caused by external circumstances, and as a result every individual has his or her own personal state of health. We should help people become capable of coping with their surroundings right down into the physical processes in their body. If someone is born into circumstances where slight muscles and nerves are appropriate, it is foolish to develop thick muscles. But where is the yardstick by which we should measure healthy development? It is within each individual human being.

Compare health with money. If we seek to make money in order to use it for charitable purposes, then it is beneficial and good. Making money is not inherently objectionable, for money enables us to help culture progress. But to go after money for its own sake is absurd, ridiculous. The same applies to good health. To strive for good health for its own sake is meaningless, but it is perfectly reasonable to strive for good health for the sake of what we can achieve through being well.

If you want to make money you should first ask yourself how much you need and then aim to make that amount. If you

want good health you should take into account what is meant
by those easily misunderstood words: well-being, love of life,
joie de vivre. People in simple, unspoilt circumstances possess
joie de vivre, love of life, enthusiasm for life. If a person whose
outer and inner life are in harmony feels listless or has a pain
either in body or soul, this should be taken as a sign of some
illness or disharmony. In public education on these subjects it
is important not to conform to stereotypes but to work out of
the whole breadth of culture in order to help people achieve
joy and satisfaction in their lives.

You might find it strange to hear a representative of spiritual science say such a thing. Surely spiritual science is usually
charged with asceticism and spoiling the fun! People who take
pleasure in a visit to the music-hall or downing eight pints of
beer every night do tend to think that individuals who enjoy
higher things are mortifying themselves. Actually those individuals would be mortifying themselves if they were to join the
party at the music-hall. Those who enjoy the music-hall
should go there, and it would be absurd to deprive them of
their fun. This would only be healthy if one were to wean
them off their taste for such things.

The efforts we make should be directed to purifying our
pleasures and satisfactions. Anthroposophists do not meet
because they find it painful to talk about higher worlds but
because this gives them the greatest pleasure. For them it
would mean deprivation of the first order if they had to sit
down and play poker together. They live as they do precisely
because they are full of *joie de vivre* in every fibre of their being.

As far as good health is concerned there is no point in laying
down rules as to what one should or should not do. What
matters is to see to it that joy and satisfaction are achieved. In
this sense those who study spiritual science are accomplished
epicures as far as life is concerned. How can we apply this to

health? In giving advice about health we must make sure of hitting on something that will please the person's astral body, give it pleasure and delight, for it is the astral body that affects the other aspects of the human being, the other bodies. Since this is easier said than done, here is an example.

Even amongst anthroposophists there are those who mortify their flesh by not eating meat any longer. For people who still have a craving for meat, becoming a vegetarian is at best merely a preparation for a later condition. Some, however, achieve a relationship with their environment that makes it impossible for them to eat meat. There was a physician who did not eat meat, not because he was an anthroposophist but because he felt that this was good for one's health. Asked by a friend why he no longer ate meat he countered with another question: 'Why don't you eat horse-flesh or cat-flesh?' The friend said that he would find this disgusting even though he was quite happy to eat pork, beef and so on. To the physician all meat was disgusting.

Only when one's inner subjective condition corresponds to the objective facts has the point been reached when external facts become health-giving. We have to be able to cope with the external facts. This is expressed by the words 'comfortable feeling' which we should not use lightly but rather in their dignified meaning of a harmonious concord of our inner forces. Happiness and joy, delight and satisfaction are the foundation of a healthy life, and they always spring from the same foundation, which is the feeling of an inner life that accompanies creativity, inner activity. The human being is happy when he can be active, but I do not mean a coarse kind of activity.

Why does love make us happy? Because it is an activity, although we often do not regard it as such. It is an activity going outwards from the inside, enveloping the other in its embrace. With it we let our inner being flow out. That is why love heals and brings happiness. Creativity can be most intimate; it need not be impetuously visible. If you are immersed in a book and the impressions from it depress you or overwhelm you, you will gradually get downhearted. But if the book awakens pictures in you, then this is a creative activity that makes for happiness. This is quite similar to turning pale when you are frightened of some event. Your blood rushes inwards in order to make you strong so that you can create an inner counterbalance to what is coming at you from outside. The feeling of fear awakens your inner creativity, making it active towards the outside. Healing comes from being aware of an inner activity. If the human being had been able to feel the inner creative activity of the eye coming into being out of the undifferentiated organ, this would have given him a sense of well-being. However, human beings were not yet conscious when that was happening.

Instead of taking a worn-out person to a sanatorium, it is much better to bring him to an environment where he can experience enjoyment, soul enjoyment at first, but then also bodily enjoyment. To be in an environment that gives you joy, where every step you take awakens enjoyment, where you see the sunlight dappling through the trees, see the colours and smell the fragrance of the flowers, this is what makes you well. But you yourself must sense this, so that you can take your own recovery in hand. Every step you take ought to stimulate inner activity. Paracelsus put this beautifully by saying: 'Each should be himself, belong to himself and to no other.'[5] Even the act of consulting someone else about our health amounts to a limitation of the powers that make us healthy. We come up against external impressions that may well appear to help for a while but will in the end lead to hysteria.

Looking at the matter in this way helps us move on to

further healthy thoughts. There are people today, especially 'lay' practitioners, who battle against conventional medicine. A reform of medicine is certainly necessary, but this is not the way to go about it. What we need is for the thoughts of spiritual science to make their way into medical science. Spiritual science does not promote amateurishness. Some people suffer from an itch to cure others, and for such people it is not difficult to find something wrong with a patient. One of the patient's organs does not look quite like the same organ in someone else; or a person breathes differently from the way the practitioner thinks everyone should breathe. So let's find a cure! Actually this is quite shocking, for it is pointless to work towards a blanket concept of what good health is. It is easy to see when something is really unhealthy, for example when someone has lost a leg through being run over. He is certainly more ill than someone whose breathing is irregular because his lungs are affected. But it is not a question of curing such a person. Just try to make him grow another leg! What needs to be done is to make his life as bearable as possible.

This applies to cases of outer illness, but also to more subtle ones. Most people have some small flaw or other, but rather than removing the flaw, why not try to help them live with it by making their life as bearable as possible? Think of a wound on a tree trunk and how the tissues and bark grow round it. It is the same with a human being. The forces of nature maintain life by growing round the flaw. 'Lay' practitioners in particular are prone to make the mistake of wanting to cure everything. They want to cultivate a single form of good health for everyone. But there is no such thing as a single form of good health, just as there is not a single normal human being. Illness and good health are both individual matters.

Whether we are a physician or a counsellor, the best thing we can do for someone is give him the firm conviction that he

will feel comfortable when he is well and uncomfortable when
he is ill. As things are nowadays this is not at all easy.
Someone who understands these things will be most wary of
illnesses that do not manifest in tiredness or pain. That is why
it is detrimental to sedate oneself with morphine. It is healthy
if good health generates zest and illness apathy. But we can
only achieve this healthy attitude to living if we make ourselves inwardly strong, which we can do by setting a strong
inner life against complicated outer circumstances. The
feverish pursuit of health will only abate when people stop
striving to achieve good health for its own sake, when they
learn to sense whether they are well, and discover that lack of
well-being can quite easily be tolerated. This can only be
achieved through having a strong world conception that is
effective right down into one's physical body. Such a conception or world view makes for harmony when it is one that
does not depend on outer impressions. The world conception
based on spiritual science leads us into realms we can only
fathom by being active with our inner being. You cannot read
a book about spiritual science as you read other books. It must
be written in a way that stimulates your own inner activity.
The more you have to struggle with it, the more you have to
read between the lines, the healthier it is. Spiritual science is
effective in all areas.

Spiritual science exists in order to become effective as a
strong spiritual movement bringing up concepts furnished
with the strongest energies that can enable us to confront what
our eyes show us. Spiritual science wants to generate an inner
life that reaches right down into limbs and blood circulation.
This will enable us all to get a feel for our own good health
through our sense of joy, pleasure and satisfaction.

Most dietary regimes are worthless, for it is not a matter of
being told by someone else what is good for me. The

important thing is to enjoy a sense of satisfaction through what I eat. We need to understand how we relate to one foodstuff or another. We should know about the spiritual process that is taking place between nature and ourselves. To make everything spiritual is what generates good health.

Some might think that a student of spiritual science would be indifferent to what he eats, unconcernedly swallowing down whatever comes to hand. To become aware of what it means to imbibe a portion of the cosmos drenched in sunlight, to know about the way our environment is related to the spiritual world, to savour it not only physically but also spiritually—this is what liberates us from sickening disgust, from stress that makes us ill.

We see what a challenge it is for human beings to guide the pursuit of health on to the right track. But spiritual science will make them strong. Every individual who turns to it will increasingly be helped to become his own yardstick. This effort to attain freedom is what comes from spiritual science; it makes us our own master. Every human being is an individual as regards his own characteristics and as regards his own states of good health and illness. We have been placed among the natural laws of the world and must get to know how we relate to this world. No power outside of ourselves can help us. Not until we have found our own inner firmness shall we be whole human beings. Nothing can then be taken away from us, but likewise nothing can be given to us. We shall find our own way with regard to good health and illness through having this strong inner firmness. This mystery of a healthy inner life of effort was put into words by a spirit whose thinking and feeling were eminently healthy. In his poem 'Primal Orphic Words' Goethe described how a harmonious human being will unerringly tread his or her own individual path:[6]

As stood the sun to the salute of planets
Upon the day that gave you to the earth,
You grew forthwith, and prospered; in your growing
Heeded the law presiding at your birth.
Sibyls and prophets told it: You must be
None but yourself, from self you cannot flee.
No time there is, no power, can decompose
The minted form that lives and living grows.

PART THREE:

LUCK, DESTINY AND THE TRIALS OF
MODERN LIFE

5. Luck—Reality and Illusion[1]

Amongst all the conclusions reached in spiritual science our contemporaries are least convinced by the conception of repeated lives on earth; and beyond this they find it hard to accept the idea that the causes a human being generates in one life echo on in subsequent lives. We call this the law of spiritual causation, or the law of karma. People deny or doubt such ideas because of the way their thought processes have been formed by life as it is today; their habits of thought will have to change before there can be any likelihood of such basic truths of spiritual science being found more widely convincing. Nevertheless, a change in today's habits of thought may gradually occur as people begin to look with unprejudiced eyes at the riddles everyday life confronts us with, riddles that can only be explained on the basis of those great truths of spiritual science, which will then come to be found more convincing.

Good luck and bad luck, concepts with so many meanings, are surely among the phenomena to be included here.[2] To someone with sensitive discernment these two terms show us the boundary that exists between what we can know and what goes on in the world around us. They also evoke an intense longing to know something about the inexplicable aspects of life, a longing that we keep on denying because we feel we ought to have a more enlightened attitude, yet which we cannot help recognizing as a perfectly natural wish. Consider how enigmatic good luck and bad luck—especially the latter—can be in a person's life. Such riddles cannot be resolved by one theoretical answer or another. They call for more than a theory, more than what may be termed abstract science. Human beings have a desire in their soul to live in some degree of harmony with their environment. But they express great disharmony if they admit—or if others say about them—that their whole life is plagued by bad luck. Such an admission has to be accompanied by a 'Why?' that is deeply significant for all we have to say about the value of human life and the value of those forces on which human life is founded.

Among the prose essays of that important but unfortunately all too little appreciated nineteenth-century poet Robert Hamerling there is one about luck.[3] It begins with a memory he says always assailed him when he pondered the question of luck, the memory of a story—be it legend or whatever—he says he heard in Vienna.

A daughter was born to a married couple. The wife died in childbirth. The same day the father heard that all his wealth had been lost at sea. The shock brought on a stroke which led to his death, too, on the day the child was born. Thus this child met with the ill luck of being an orphan from the day she entered earthly existence. Initially she was taken in by a rich relative who made a will leaving her a large fortune. But this relative died when the child was still quite young, and when the will was opened it was found to contain a technical error. It was contested, and the child lost the fortune that had been intended for her. She grew up in want and poverty and later had to earn her living working as a maidservant. A very kind, nice young lad whom the girl liked very much fell in love with her. But after they had been walking out for a while, so that having trodden a path through ill luck and most difficult circumstances the girl might have begun to hope for some sort of happiness, it turned out that her lover was Jewish, which meant that there could be no marriage. She reproached him bitterly for having deceived her, yet could not bring herself to part from him. There are always such strange alternations in life. The lad likewise could not part from her and promised that when his father died, which was expected to happen quite soon, he would be baptized, and then they could get married. Sure enough, he was soon called to his father's deathbed. Then, to add to all the troubles suffered by this unfortunate young woman, she became very ill indeed. Meanwhile the father of her betrothed had passed away elsewhere, and the young man had been baptized. But when he came to the girl she had already died of the mental suffering she had endured, combined with her physical illness. All he found was a lifeless bride. He was overcome by the bitterest grief. He could not help himself, but he must look upon her face once more although she was already buried. He managed to obtain permission for this. But just imagine, the position of her body showed that she must have been buried alive and tried to turn in her grave on coming to her senses!

Hamerling says he always remembered this story when there was talk of excessively bad luck, for it can certainly seem as though a person is pursued by ill luck from cradle to grave and even beyond the grave, as in this instance. Perhaps this is a made-up story, but we can surely all agree that such events are possible, whether they actually happened or not. The story illustrates very clearly the disquieting question: 'Why? What is the value of a life so plagued by ill luck?'

This leads us to ask whether it is possible to speak about good luck and bad luck at all in the context of a single life on earth. Our ordinary habits of thought might at least be challenged to look beyond such a single life if it is one that appears so enmeshed in the world that to live its span between birth and death seems to be without value. In such a case we may feel impelled to look beyond the limits set by birth and death.

Examining the terms 'good luck' and 'bad luck' more

closely, we immediately realize that in fact they apply only to one specific sphere. There are many things in the world outside us that are analogous with our own accord or discord with the world, but in these similar situations not involving human beings we are scarcely likely to speak about good or bad luck. Look at a crystal that is supposed to create regular shapes in accordance with specific laws of nature. By preventing it from forming the angles and edges it ought to have, other nearby crystals or forces of nature can compel it not to develop fully. There are in fact very few crystals in nature perfectly formed in accordance with their inner laws. Or consider a plant that also has innate formative laws. How many plants are prevented by wind and weather and all kinds of other things in their environment from unfolding the full force of their inner formative impulse! And the same can be said of animals. It is an undeniable fact that many, many embryos of living creatures are hardly created before they perish without reaching any real development because existing conditions make it impossible for them to fulfil their potential. Think of the vast number of spawn that have the potential of inhabiting the ocean, yet how few actually live and grow. Although the creatures we find in the different kingdoms of nature quite obviously possess innate formative forces and laws, we have to admit that these innate formative forces and laws are up against limitations in their surroundings that make it impossible for those creatures to live in harmony with their environment.

We cannot overlook the fact that something similar is at play in the good or bad luck confronting human beings. Look how some individuals are confronted by endless hindrances preventing them from fulfilling their potential. See how fortunate others are in being able—like crystals, metaphorically speaking—freely to shape all their edges and angles, saying:

'There is nothing in my way; external circumstances, the ways of the world, all obligingly help me in developing my inner potential to the full!'

The latter instance alone is regarded as good luck. Anything else either meets with indifference or compels us to talk of bad luck. Yet in the case of crystals, or plants, or the myriad spawn perishing in the ocean before even being born, we cannot speak of bad luck except in a strictly metaphorical sense, or if we succumb to fanciful ideas. We feel we have to rise to the level of human life before we can justifiably speak of bad or good luck. It is also noticeable that there is a borderline beyond which the ideas of good or bad luck do not apply even in situations where a human life appears to be hemmed in or destroyed from every side. Do we speak of bad luck—we can sense that we do not—in the case of a martyr condemned to death by authorities opposed to the message he brings to the world? Is it justifiable to say that it was Giordano Bruno's bad luck to be burned at the stake?[4] We feel that there is a limit within the human being beyond which it becomes impossible to speak simply of bad luck—or of good luck when some project is successful. Having established that good or bad luck belongs solely to the human sphere, we find that within that sphere it covers an even narrower span.

Looking at individual human beings and what they themselves feel about their life ranged between good and bad luck, we discover how little we are able to pin down this good or bad luck in definite terms. Consider Diogenes when Alexander the Great urged him to ask for a favour, in other words for some good luck—again, this may be a legend, but it could have happened. Not many in his situation would have done this, but Diogenes asked Alexander to move out of his light.[5] So that was what he found lacking in his happiness at that moment. What would most other people have interpreted as lacking in their happiness at such a moment? But let us continue. Take a pleasure-seeker who only regards his life as fortunate if all the desires arising from his passions and instincts can be satisfied, sometimes by the most banal of pleasures. Could one ever regard what such a person would consider lucky as also being lucky for an ascetic, for someone who expects to perfect himself—and only considers life worth living if he can do this—by denying himself all kinds of things or even subjecting himself to pain and anguish that would not ordinarily be inflicted on him by luck, either good or bad?

So an ascetic and a pleasure-seeker have entirely different concepts of good and bad luck. Yet we can go still further in showing how any generalized concept of luck must of necessity elude our grasp. Think how deeply unhappy a person can be who for no good reason, without any foundation in reality, becomes fiercely jealous. There are no grounds for this person's jealousy and yet he imagines he has all kinds of reasons. He is unhappy in the profoundest sense without any external reason. The degree, the intensity of his unhappiness does not depend on any outer reality; it results solely from the manner in which the person relates to the outer reality of his life, in this case a complete illusion.

In a charming tale at the beginning of the first volume of his *Flegeljahre* Jean Paul has shown how bad luck as well as good luck can be highly subjective, turning our attention at every step away from the outer and towards the inner world.[6] A man who normally lives in the middle of Germany pictures to himself how fortunate it would be for him to be a parson in Sweden. There is a delightful passage where he imagines himself in his parsonage as the day arrives when it grows dark at two o'clock in the afternoon. He sees the people going to church each with his or her own lantern. This conjures up pictures from his childhood when his brothers and sisters once all came along, each carrying a lantern. He revels in this inner picture of the people going to church in the darkness, each carrying a lantern. Or he dreams his way into other situations called up simply by memories linked to certain natural scenes; for instance if he imagines himself in Italy he can almost see the orange trees, and so on. All this generates in him a mood of wonderful happiness, yet nothing is real; it is all a dream.

With this dream of being a parson in Sweden Jean Paul is undoubtedly pointing to profound aspects of good and bad luck by showing how they can be diverted away from the outer world and into our inner being. So now, since good and bad luck can depend entirely on our inner life, we see any generalized concept of luck melting away before our eyes. Yet when you look at what people usually call their good or their bad luck you realize that in countless instances they are referring not to their inner life but to something external. You could even say that the specific quality of our desire for good luck is deeply rooted in our constant longing not to be alone with our thoughts, our feelings and all our inner being, but to be in harmony with all that works and weaves in our environment.

We speak of good luck when we do not want the success or influence we enjoy to depend on us alone; we attach importance to it being caused not by us but by something outside us. Consider the luck of the gambler—for the same applies to trifling as well as to great things. Although it may appear paradoxical, we can quite easily compare the luck of the gambler with the satisfaction we gain when we achieve an understanding of something. When we arrive at an understanding of something, this makes us feel that our thinking and our life of soul are in harmony with the world, that we comprehend inwardly what is outside us, that we are not alone with the world staring us in the face like a riddle, but that our inner being responds to what is outside us.

The satisfaction we gain when we achieve an understanding of something derives from our having a lively, intimate contact with what is outside us; it arises from the way something external lights up within us and finds itself mirrored there; it comes about when what is outside finds links with what is inside, as is proved by the harmony between the two. Similarly, if we want to analyse the satisfaction of a successful gambler we have to admit—even if he himself does not question the reason for it—that he would not be satisfied to the same degree if his results were achieved solely through his own efforts. His satisfaction arises from the way something is brought about from outside, without his assistance. It arises from the way the world, as it were, takes account of him, giving him something advantageous and demonstrating that in his individual case he is not outside it but has a specific relationship, a definite link with it. The feeling of misfortune a gambler has when he loses emanates from the lack of that sense of belonging to the world; his bad luck generates a sense of being shut out by a world that takes no account of him—as though his contact with it had been broken off.

In short, we see that what we mean by good or bad luck is not something restricted to our own inner being but something that has most profoundly to do with bringing about links between ourselves and the world. Hence there is hardly anything in these enlightened times about which we can so easily become superstitious, grotesquely superstitious, as what we call our good luck, our expectation directed towards some kind of force or element that lies outside ourselves and is supposed to come to our assistance. People get exceedingly superstitious about such things.

I used to know a very enlightened German writer. At the

time of which I speak he was writing a play. Although he knew perfectly well that his play would not be finished by the end of a particular month, he had the superstition that it would only be successful if he sent it to the relevant theatre director before the first day of the subsequent month. If it arrived later, his superstition told him, it would fail. One day, towards the end of that month, I happened to be walking in the street when I saw him bicycling in hot haste to the post office. Through my friendship with him I knew that his play was far from finished, so I waited for him to come out. 'I have sent my play to the theatre,' he said. 'Is it finished, then?' I asked. He replied, 'I still have some work to do on the last act, but I have sent it in now because I believe it can only be successful if it arrives before the end of this month. I have written, though, asking them to return it to me when it arrives, so that I can then finish it. But it simply had to be sent in now.'

This is an example of how an individual does not rely on his own capabilities but expects help from outside; he assumes that he cannot by himself, by his own hard work and ability, bring about what he hopes will happen; instead the world outside himself will come to his assistance because that world has some interest in him; this makes him feel less lonely than he would feel as an isolated soul.

All this only goes to show how the concept of luck as a generality slips through our fingers when we try to grasp hold of it. It also eludes us when we look for references about it in literature, for people who write often allude to such things. Everyone knows, however, that one can only speak correctly about matters to which one relates in a living way rather than merely through theory.

Philosophers or psychologists who write about luck are as a rule only connected in a living way with the good or bad luck they have themselves experienced. There is, moreover, one factor that weighs very heavily in the balance, and that is that cognition as such, in the way we encounter it in the world of human beings around us—knowledge and knowing as such, if it is of a more elevated kind—in itself signifies a kind of happiness. Anyone who has ever felt the inner delight knowledge can give will admit this; and it is also attested to by the way the most eminent philosophers, from Aristotle right up to our own time, have always described the possession of wisdom, of knowledge, as especially fortunate.

On the other hand, however, we must also ask whether such an answer to the question of what good luck is can have any meaning for someone who works in the dark down a mine week in week out, with hardly a break, or for someone buried alive down a mine and having to survive for many days in the most ghastly circumstances. What has such a philosophical interpretation of good luck got to do with what lives in the soul of someone whose task in life is menial or repulsive?

Life gives strange answers to the question of what good luck is. We have abundant experience to show that the answers philosophers give in this connection are often grotesquely remote from what meets us in everyday life provided we consider this life in its true character. Life also teaches us something else with regard to luck, and here life itself appears as a noteworthy contradiction to commonly accepted notions of good luck. One case may serve as an example for many.

Think of someone with high ideals and even the gift of an exceptional imagination who has to do the humble work of a common soldier for most of his life. I speak of a case that is no legend but the life of a most remarkable man, Josef Emanuel Hilscher, who was born in Austria in 1804 and died in 1837. For most of his life he served as a common soldier, never rising above the rank of quartermaster despite his brilliant gifts. This man left behind a large number of poems not only perfect in form but filled with a deep life of soul, and also excellent translations of Byron's poems. He had a rich inner life. Picture the complete contrast between what the day brought him by way of luck and his inner life. His poems are by no means steeped in pessimism; they are full of strength and exuberance. They show us how his life—in spite of many a disappointment inherent in it—expanded to encompass an infinity and attained a level of inner happiness. It is a pity that humanity as a whole so easily forgets such manifestations, for when we look more closely at a phenomenon like this we are reminded—since of course such things are only a matter of degrees—that in a life that appears to be entirely devoid of happiness it is perhaps possible for a human being to create a situation of happiness out of his own inmost being.

If you want to cling to easily misunderstood or over-simplified ideas, it is possible, from the point of view of spiritual science in particular, to fulminate fanatically against good luck, and also to want to explain life on the basis of repeated earth lives and karma in a fanatically one-sided manner. One way of fulminating against good luck on the basis of spiritual science would be to deduce that since spiritual science aims to raise human beings above egoism one must consider any efforts to find happiness and contentment as amounting to nothing but egoism. Even a great man like Aristotle, however, thought it ridiculous to maintain that a virtuous individual could somehow be contented in the midst of inexplicable suffering.[7] Good luck need not be regarded solely as satisfied egoism, for even if this is what it is in the first place it need not be without value for humanity as a whole. The happiness of good luck can also be interpreted as bringing all our soul forces into a harmonious mood, thus enabling them to unfold in every direction, whereas the unhappiness of bad luck creates disharmonious moods in our soul life, thus preventing us from making the most of our capacities and strengths. So we can regard good luck, even if we initially see it as merely the satisfaction of egoism, as being the promoter of inner soul harmony, and can on the one hand hope that those on whom good luck bestows an inner harmony of soul forces will gradually transcend their egoism, whereas someone pursued by bad luck will find it hard to transcend it. On the other hand we can also say that someone who seeks after good luck and receives it as the satisfaction of his egoism can then also work for his own good as well as that of others because his forces are brought into harmony by it.

So we should not fulminate one-sidedly against what we call good luck. On the other hand another mistake is also made by some who believe themselves to be quite close to spiritual science even when they have merely picked up one snippet or another from afar. These people say: 'Here is an unfortunate individual and there is a fortunate one; if I consider karma and the way one life is determined by another, I can easily explain how the unfortunate individual prepared his own unhappiness in a past life, and how the fortunate one brought about his own happiness through an earlier life.' A statement like this can be rather insidious because to some extent it is correct. Karma—the law concerning the determining of one life out of another—must, however, not be taken to be a merely explanatory law. It must be regarded as something that penetrates into our will, causing us to live in accordance with that law. The law is only justified and vindicated if it enhances and enriches life.

With regard to good luck, we have seen that initially human beings generate their addiction to happiness out of a desire not to be alone but to possess something of the external conditions of the world in such a way that these take an interest in them. On the other hand we have also seen that the happiness of good luck can be entirely at variance with external circumstances and come into being solely through a person's views, through what he makes out of his experience of those circumstances.

Where can we find a solution—arising not out of abstractions and theories but out of reality—to this seeming contradiction? We can find the solution if we turn our inner vision to what may be called the inmost core of man's being. In earlier lectures[8] we showed how this inmost core works on the outer human being, shaping even his physical body, and how it also places him into his proper situation in the world. In following up this conception of the inner core by asking ourselves how it can relate to the good or bad luck experienced by an individual, we most readily find an answer if we consider that some stroke of good luck may so affect his inner core that the individual begins to say: 'I intended this, I willed it; I used my good sense, my wisdom, in such a way that this should come about; but now I realize that the result, this success of mine, far exceeds what I initiated through my cleverness, what I predetermined or what I was able to foresee.'

What individual, especially someone in a responsible position in the world, would not admit in numerous situations that the degree of success he has achieved far outweighs the effort he put in? If you regard man's inner core as something that is there not just for once, as something that is in the process of a long evolution in the sense of spiritual science, you can see this inner core shaping not just one life but many, including this one that is our immediate present. When this inner core of man's being passes through the gate of death it then proceeds through a supersensible world, returning again when the time comes to be active in physical life in a new existence. What attitude can an individual adopt who comprehends his own central core in this way, understanding himself within a world-conception of this kind? What attitude can he adopt towards the type of success that drops into his lap in the way we have described?

He will certainly not say: 'This has been my good luck and therefore I am satisfied; with the degree of effort I made I expected rather less, but I am pleased that my good luck has granted me greater success.' Someone who seriously believes in karma and in repeated lives on earth, and who strives to lead his life in accordance with karma, will never say such a thing. He will say: 'The success is there but I myself have proved feeble in comparison with it; rather than be content with this success I shall learn from it how to redouble my efforts; I will sow new seeds in my inmost core so that they may lead it on to ever higher perfection; my unmerited success, my lucky chance, has shown me where I am lacking, so I must learn from it.'

A person who meets with good luck in success and who sees karma in the correct light and believes in it can give no other response than this. How will he deal with such a lucky chance? (I mean chance in the sense of something unexpectedly dropping into one's lap.) Such a person will consider it not as an end but as a beginning, a beginning from which he will learn and which will cast its light forward into subsequent phases of his existence.

What is the converse of this? Let us look at it squarely. Someone who believes in repeated earth-lives, or in karma, or in spiritual causes, will receive new seeds with which to spur on his strength through regarding his lucky success as a beginning, as the cause of his further development; and the converse of this would be not to regard a misfortune, a failure merely as a blow that has befallen us. A person who looks beyond the isolated experience will take the misfortune as an end, something final, something of which the cause must be sought in the past, just as the effects of a success must be sought in the future, in the future of our own development. We regard the misfortune as an effect of our own development. How can this be?

We can make this clear by using a comparison showing that we are not always good judges of causes in life. Suppose someone has lived a life of carefree idleness on his father's money up to the age of 18, enjoying from his own point of view a very happy existence. When he is 18 his father loses all his wealth, so now the son is obliged to train for a proper job instead of idling away his time. Initially this causes him all kinds of grief and anguish and he bemoans his fate: 'Alas, such bad luck has befallen me,' he says. It is questionable, however, whether he is really the best judge of his destiny in this situation. If he learns a useful occupation now, perhaps when he is 50 we will say: 'Well, at the time I regarded it as very bad luck when my father lost all his wealth, but now I can only see it as bad luck for my father, not for myself; if this bad luck had not befallen me I may have remained a good-for-nothing all my life, whereas as things turned out I became a useful member of society—I became what I am now.'

So when is this man a good judge of his destiny? Is it at 18, when the bad luck befalls him, or at 50, as he looks back at that bad luck? Suppose he thinks further and enquires after the cause of the bad luck. He might very well say to himself: 'It was really quite unnecessary for me to consider myself unlucky at that time. Regarded superficially it appears that I was struck by bad luck because my father lost his wealth. But suppose that from my earliest childhood I had been zealous in my desire for knowledge and had learnt a huge amount without any compulsion from outside, so that my father's bad luck would not have inconvenienced me at all. In that case the transition would have been quite different and what befell me would not have been bad luck. Though it may appear that the reason for my bad luck lay outside me, in actual fact its deeper cause came from within. It was because of the way I was that what happened became a misfortune for me, bringing with it much anguish and grief. I attracted the bad luck to myself.'

Somebody reaching this conclusion has begun to understand that everything approaching us from outside is indeed attracted from within and that we may regard what is thus attracted to us as being brought about by our own development. Every misfortune can be represented as being the result of some imperfection in ourselves; it indicates that something in us is not as perfect as it should be. Bad luck is the converse of success; we comprehend bad luck as an effect, an end-product of what was caused by our self in earlier periods of our development. So by turning to the inmost core of our being, if we seriously believe the cause of bad luck to lie in our various lives on earth, in karma, and therefore stop blaming it on outer circumstance, we shall find in it a challenge to make ourselves ever more perfect, to learn from life, to regard life as a school. Then, if we look at things in this light, karma and what we term the law of repeated earth-lives will become for us a force for life, for all that makes life richer and more meaningful.

We may well ask: 'Can mere knowledge about the law of karma by itself enhance life, make it richer and more meaningful? Can this in itself perhaps turn bad luck into good luck in some way?' Though it may seem strange to many these days, nevertheless I should like to say something that may be significant for a full comprehension of good and bad luck from the point of view of spiritual science.

Let us recall Hamerling's tale of the young girl whose bad luck followed her up to her death and even beyond the grave when she was buried alive. This may sound peculiar to someone who has not examined closely what strength can arise from knowledge, but let us hypothetically imagine the unfortunate young woman transported to an environment in which a spiritual world view is accepted to a degree that leads individuals to say: 'In my being there lives a central core that transcends birth and death, that shows the effects of past earth-lives in what it now is, and that gathers strength for new earth-lives in the future.' Let us imagine that this knowledge became strength in the soul of the young woman—for it is conceivable, after all, that such ideas might have been present in her. Such ideas increase one's belief in the strength of one's own central core of being, so we can say: 'The strength that emanates from spirit and soul works on the body from that central core of being.' This will be shown in the coming lectures from other points of view.[9] In this way it could well have beneficially affected the young woman's state of health; the strength derived from such beliefs might have sustained her until her friend returned after his father's death. This may appear odd to many who are not aware of the power such knowledge has, knowledge that stems from genuine reality and is therefore neither abstract nor merely theoretical, knowledge that works like a seed force growing in the soul.

So we see that in matters of luck there is not necessarily a need to console those who have to spend their whole life doing work that can never satisfy them and whose expectations of life are rejected as long as they live. We notice instead that in fact something like an awakening of strength can come from a strong belief in the central core of the human being which knows that this single life is one of many. Through my links with the world as a whole, within which I have my place, and through the way I take hold of myself spiritually, something becomes explicable for me in my inmost soul, something that initially confronted me as my seeming good or bad luck, the good or bad destiny in my life. Ordinary consolation cannot help us overcome what we consider to be a real misfortune. The only thing that can comfort us is being able to regard what befalls us as one link in the chain of existence. Then we see that to consider one life alone is to consider merely the appearance and not the reality, just as someone who has idled away his time up to the age of 18, when he suffers the bad luck I described and has to begin working, is only considering the appearance if he regards this as a genuine misfortune instead of the cause of subsequent good fortune.

When we thus look more deeply into these things we do indeed come to realize that regarding matters of luck from a narrow angle can only show us the appearance, and that we discover the true significance and essence of good and bad luck if we place them in the context of our whole existence. If we were to regard our whole existence as consisting merely of our life between birth and death, then we should never be able to find an explanation for a human life that yields no satisfaction whatsoever, either in day-to-day existence or in the work a person has to do. We can only find an explanation through the reality of human destiny as described by spiritual science, through which we know that once we comprehend something it no longer has power over us. An individual whose central core takes a stroke of good luck as an encouragement for onward development will also regard a stroke of bad luck as a challenge to develop further. So the seeming contradiction is resolved when we turn from the attitude that regards good or bad luck as something coming to us from outside and pay attention instead to how we can transform these experiences inwardly and what we can make out of them.

Having learnt from the law of karma not merely to draw

satisfaction from success but to regard it also as a challenge to develop further, we then also learn to regard failure and bad luck in a similar light. Everything is transformed in the human soul, so that what has the appearance of good or bad luck is transformed into a reality there.

This implies much that is immensely important. Think, for instance, of a person who rejects outright the idea of repeated earth-lives. This person might see someone suffering from unfounded jealousy based on an imagined situation, or perhaps someone falling under the spell of an illusory happiness; or he might see someone else developing a definite inner reality—something most real for his inner life—merely out of his imagination, that is, out of mere semblance, not out of the world of real facts. The person might then after all reach the conclusion: 'Surely, with regard to the human being's inner life in its relation to the external world, it would be unbelievably inappropriate to presume that this matter ends here, in this one life?'

When an individual passes through the gate of death the things he links with reality here on earth, such as jealousy or an illusion of happiness, are blotted out. Things that have united with his soul through joy and sorrow, however, feelings that have arisen as effects of being deeply moved, these things have become a force in his soul, a force that lives in his soul and plays a part in his further development in the world. So the transformation described shows us that human beings are indeed called upon to develop their own reality out of appearances.

This also gives us the explanation for what we said at the beginning, namely, that a person's relationship with luck is such that he can definitely not unite it with his own 'I', with his own individuality. Since he cannot directly unite with his 'I' these external happenings that come upon him and enhance his life, he can instead take the luck into his inner being so that what was initially external appearance becomes inner reality. In this way such a person transforms external appearance into being, into reality.

We saw earlier how crystals, plants and animals are similarly not able to fulfil the potential of their inner laws of form; we mentioned how external factors hinder them in this. We saw how countless spawn have to perish before they can properly come into being. In which way are these different? Why is it that in these cases we cannot speak of good or bad luck? It is because in these cases it is not a matter of something external becoming internal through being mirrored internally in such a way that appearances are transformed into genuine existence.

It is solely through having a central core of being that we humans can detach ourselves from the reality of our immediate external surroundings and experience a new reality. This reality that we experience within us differs from ordinary life because we can say: 'On the one hand I live in a line of heredity through carrying in me what I have inherited from my parents, grandparents and so on; but I also live in a purely spiritual line of causation that gives me something over and above whatever luck the external world has in store for me.' It is this alone that shows how human beings belong to two worlds, an external one and an internal one. You may call this dualism, but the very way in which we transform appearance into being, into reality, shows that this dualism, too, is merely an appearance, since in us outer appearance is continually being transformed into inner reality. Life also shows us that what we experience in our imagination when we interpret facts wrongly also becomes reality within us.

So now we see that what we call good or bad luck is closely bound up with our inner human being. We also see that it is closely bound up with that inner core of our being which is hinted at when spiritual science speaks of a succession of lives on earth. We might well ask: 'Are we, then, basing all the external semblance of luck on another, inner, luck which we should include as something permanent in our development?' External luck is wonderfully characterized in the legend of Croesus when Solon tells Croesus that one should never count one's life happy until its end, for all external luck can change. Good luck can turn into bad. Which part of luck can never be taken away from us? It is what we make of that luck, whether it be the result of success or failure. Our relationship with good as well as bad luck is summed up perfectly in that good old saying about each one of us forging our own luck.

There are many excellent and apt folk sayings about luck, sayings that show what profound philosophy there is even in the simplest man's outlook. Many a highly educated individual could learn a tremendous amount from such sayings. Some truths, though, are couched in rather uncouth terms, for example the one about a certain human characteristic against which even the gods themselves contend in vain.[10] This is offset by another saying that points to this very characteristic—against which the gods are supposed to contend in vain—by stating that fools have the most luck. We need not conclude from this that the gods seek to bribe such people with good luck to make up for their stupidity. Nevertheless, a saying like this reveals an awareness of inner depths and of the need to deepen our understanding of what we must call the inner links between human being and luck in the outer world. So long as our wisdom is directed solely to outer things in all their aspects it will be of little use to us. It will serve us only when it has become inner wisdom, when it has regained the quality that primal, unspoilt human beings still have, when it is built on the strong central core of man's inwardness that transcends birth and death and can only be explained by being considered in the light of repeated lives on earth.

Thus what we experience as luck arising only from the outer world, luck that is merely an appearance, has to be distinguished from what we call the true being of luck which only comes into existence once we manage to make something of life's outer circumstances, transforming them, absorbing them into the developing core of our being that progresses from one life to the next. Then we understand why someone assailed by frightful physical pain—Herder—can say to his son, 'Give me one sublime and beautiful thought that I may refresh myself by it!'[11] We see clearly how Herder expects a sublime, beautiful thought to illumine his afflicted life as a refreshment, in other words as a stroke of good luck. In such an instance it is easy to say that in his inner core a human being forges his own luck.

Let us turn to the world view of spiritual science, parts of which we have been able to touch on today. We see that it is a powerful force because it is not merely theoretical knowledge. It touches our core of soul and spirit, filling it with something that transcends good and bad luck. If we can take it in this vein, then this world view, almost more than any other, furnishes us with those great thoughts that enable us, even as we succumb to bad luck, to be suffused in the knowledge: 'This is only a part of my life as a whole!'

We raised the question of luck today in order to show how these real thoughts about life as a whole, given to us by spiritual science, fire and inspire our everyday life. These thoughts intervene in life not merely as theories; they bring with them the power of life itself. This is the essential thing. We must have more than external grounds of consolation to offer someone who is supposed to learn how to bear his external ill luck by having his inner powers awakened. We must be able to give him real inner powers that lead beyond the sphere of his ill luck towards another sphere to which he also belongs even when life appears to contradict this. The only science to provide this is one that shows how human life transcends birth and death and is linked with the whole beneficent foundation of our world-order.

A world conception that is capable of this is one that provides a content for the intuitions of even the best of human beings. A world conception like this enables a human being to stand firm like someone on a ship tossed to and fro by the waves in a storm, who nevertheless finds within himself the courage to set more store by the power and being of his inner core than by anything in the world outside.

Perhaps our considerations today may serve to set before you an ideal prefigured to some extent by Goethe, a human ideal valid for all of us that goes beyond Goethe's intuition, something that is not directly achieved in a single human lifetime but is there as an ideal for man's life as a totality if an individual, tossed to and fro through life on the stormy waves of good and bad luck, can rely on his own inner power. With some slight adaptation, the insight arising from this can be expressed in Goethe's words:[12]

> Man stands with courage at the helm;
> By wind and waves the ship is driven,
> Yet these do not affect his inner being.
> Ruling them he looks into the angry depths,
> And trusts, no matter wrecked or safe in port,
> The powers of his inner being.

6. Psychological Distress and the Birth Pangs of the Consciousness Soul[1]

The truths we seek in spiritual science should become not lifeless knowledge but living wisdom that can play a part in the concerns of real life at every important juncture. Perhaps it is only natural and understandable that people still find spiritual science rather abstract, and that in consequence of this presumed abstractness the wisdom it depicts appears rather stereotyped and of little use in everyday life. Those who have so far paid little attention to it might well ask what difference it makes to know that the human being consists of so and so many bodies, or that humanity has evolved over various cultural epochs and will continue to evolve further, and so on. Spiritual science can often appear rather fruitless to those who think they have to approach life in an entirely practical way in order to cope with the demands our epoch is making on them. Indeed, even many of those who have already developed some sympathy towards it often study it in quite a fruitless manner.

Nevertheless, spiritual science is in itself immensely alive and in the long run it will—in fact, it must—come to play a part even in the most prosaic matters of everyday life. I should like to make this clear by a specific example. Let us look at something I presume we are all familiar with from spiritual science and show how it can come vividly alive if we consider it in a fresh and lively way.

Most of us have quite often dwelt on the fact that our present time was preceded by what is known as the fourth post-Atlantean epoch of culture in which the Greeks and Romans were the outstanding peoples.[2] Subsequent centuries right up to the fourteenth or fifteenth century continued to be influenced by that fourth epoch, but since the fifteenth century we have been living fully in the fifth post-Atlantean epoch of culture. This is the period of our present incarnation, and it will continue for many centuries to come. Most of us have often also dwelt on the fact that during the fourth post-Atlantean epoch of culture, the period of the Greeks and Romans, the principal element to be developed in human beings—by means of all external culture and work—was what we call the intellectual or mind soul; and that now it is the task of humanity to develop the consciousness soul.[3]

What do we mean by saying that the consciousness soul has to be developed? To understand this abstract statement correctly we have to realize that in this fifth post-Atlantean epoch of culture it applies to mankind as a whole. All the peoples must work together in this fifth post-Atlantean epoch in order to bring the consciousness soul to expression, and indeed all conditions and circumstances of life point to this being the case. If we look at life with our eyes open we find corroboration everywhere for the fact that the consciousness soul is to come to expression in our time.

The whole of human life was different in the Graeco-Roman epoch. The stage that human beings had reached during that part of the overall post-Atlantean age involved their being given the power of intellect and the power of mind and feeling. Intellect as such has many facets, but this is something that is not seen quite clearly today. The Greeks and Romans depended upon intellect in their soul in a manner that differs from what happens today in the fifth post-Atlantean epoch of culture. The Greeks and Romans received intellect—in so far as they needed it—as part of their natural capacity for development, so their situation was entirely different from ours. As the individual grew up, his natural intellect grew with him as a part of his overall natural potential. There was no need to educate this natural intellect in the way that is necessary today, and as will become increasingly necessary as the fifth post-Atlantean epoch progresses. It developed as a natural capacity, so that if people developed according to natural circumstances in a particular incarnation they either had intellect or they did not. The latter meant that there was something wrong; it was abnormal, not normal.

The situation was similar with the mind or feeling aspect. In the fourth post-Atlantean epoch the mind or feeling aspect developed in an appropriate fashion. When one person met another he knew how to adjust to that other person. History tells us little about this, but it was so. This is a particular facet of the difference between people of those earlier centuries, up to the fifteenth, and people of our own time. In those earlier centuries human beings did not pass by one another with as little interest as they so often do nowadays.

When people meet today it often takes them a long time to get to know one another properly. They have to learn all kinds of things about each other before any mutual trust can begin to form. What it takes us a long time to achieve—and even then we frequently fail—was achieved at a stroke when people met one another in former centuries, specifically in the epoch of Graeco-Roman culture. They quickly succeeded in encountering one another by virtue of their individuality, without having to spend a long time exchanging thoughts and feelings first. People got to know one another quickly in so far as this was for the mutual benefit of the two concerned, or even for the benefit of several people who perhaps wanted to form a society together. One person's mind and feeling aspect had a much more spiritual way of working on the mind and feeling aspect of another person. It was similar to the way we can recognize the colours of plants today. (In the seventh post-Atlantean epoch of culture this, too, will no longer be a matter of course; special circumstances will be necessary in order to know nature.) Today we can immediately recognize a plant without having to get to know it first. The first impression is sufficient for an ordinary person to recognize a plant; and in Graeco-Roman times this is what it was like with regard to human beings.

This was adequate for the simpler situations of life in those times. That way of getting to know the other person's mind or feeling aspect was suitable for the fourth post-Atlantean epoch. Today, however, the world is suffused in quite a different network of feeling relationships. You must take into account that by far the greatest part of people's inter-relationships in the fourth post-Atlantean epoch rested on personal encounters. The arrangements people made depended on personal meetings. Today's art of printing which has made our dealings with one another so impersonal—and will go on making them increasingly so—belongs in the fifth post-Atlantean epoch. Modern communications now bring people together in ways that detract from the benefit of forming mutual relationships at a stroke. These modern means of communication make people encounter one another in the world in a far more impersonal manner.

This is how humanity is developing now. We no longer come with a ready-made mind or feeling aspect that works instantaneously. Nor do we have a ready-made intellect that can penetrate everything. The consciousness soul is giving us something much more separate and individual, with a greater tendency towards egoism and loneliness within our own body, than was the case with the intellectual or mind soul. The consciousness soul is making human beings much more individual; they are becoming more like solitary hermits as they go about in the world than they were when the intellectual or mind soul was the dominant feature. The way human beings turn in upon themselves has already become their most salient characteristic, and they will continue to do this more and more. It is the consciousness soul that gives people this characteristic of being shut up in themselves, locked away from the rest of humanity and living in isolation. Hence it is more difficult to get to know other people, let alone achieve real familiarity or intimacy. You have to go through a complicated rigmarole of becoming acquainted before you can get on intimate terms with someone.

What is the purpose of all this? To gain some insight into it let us consider one specific truth from spiritual science which tells us that there is absolutely no question of the way we meet each other today being a matter of mere chance. The paths of our lives bring us together with certain people and not with others. This results from the effects of our individual karma, for we have entered a period of evolution that in some senses has brought to a culmination the earlier karmic developments undergone by human beings. Think how much less karma people had accumulated in earlier periods of earthly evolution. Every time we incarnate, new karma is formed. Initially people had to encounter one another under conditions that did not entail having met before, so the relationships they developed were entirely new. Having meanwhile incarnated on the earth many, many times, we have now reached a stage in which we hardly ever meet someone with whom we have not experienced one thing or another in earlier incarnations. We are brought together with others through what we experienced in earlier incarnations. Although we may appear to meet people by chance, in fact we do so as the result of meeting them in earlier incarnations, when forces were generated that now lead us to meet them again.

The consciousness soul, enclosed within itself as it should

become in our time, can only develop if what takes place today between one human being and another is less important than what is now beginning to work, hermit-like, within us—something, namely, that rises up in us as the result of earlier incarnations. When two people met in Graeco-Roman times they had to make an immediate impression on one another. Now, however, things have to be different so that the more isolated consciousness soul can develop within us. When one person meets another it is what rises up in either of them as the result of earlier incarnations that should begin to work. This takes longer to come about than an instantaneous acquaintance between the two of them based on external appearances. It means that they must allow what they experienced with each other to rise up gradually, in their feelings, in their instincts. This is what is needed today: that in getting to know one another our individualities first have to be pared down. In this kind of getting to know one another through the paring down of individuality, reminiscences and effects of earlier incarnations can rise up, as yet unconsciously and instinctively. The consciousness soul can only form when we enter into relationships with others out of our inner being. The intellectual and mind soul, on the other hand, was formed more through encounters resulting in instantaneous acquaintance.

What I have just described is as yet only in its early stages as far as the fifth post-Atlantean epoch is concerned. As this epoch progresses people will find it more and more difficult to achieve appropriate relationships with one another, for this attainment of appropriate relationships now entails the application of inner development, inner activity. This has already begun, but it will become more and more widespread and intense. Even now it is already difficult for people brought together by karma to understand one another directly. One reason is that other karmic connections may be sapping their strength, so that they lack the energy to bring to the fore instinctively everything they have in them from earlier incarnations.

People are brought together and love one another; certain influences from earlier incarnations bring this about. But then other forces work against this when reminiscences of this kind rise up, so they part again. But it is not only those who meet each other during the course of life who will have to try and find out whether what arises within them can provide sufficient basis for an ongoing relationship. Sons and daughters, too, will find it increasingly difficult to understand fathers and mothers, parents will find it harder and harder to understand their children, and the same will be the case for sisters and brothers. Mutual understanding will become increasingly difficult because it will be more and more necessary for people first of all to let what lives in them karmically emerge properly from the depths of their being.

So you see what a negative prospect is opening up for the fifth post-Atlantean epoch—the prospect of difficulties in mutual understanding amongst human beings. We are challenged to look this evolutionary necessity squarely in the face instead of remaining dreamily in the dark, for it is, in fact, entirely necessary for our evolution. If humanity in the fifth post-Atlantean epoch were not faced with this prospect of having difficulty in mutual understanding, the consciousness soul would be unable to develop. The consequence of this would be that people would have to live collectively more on the basis of natural instincts. The individual aspects of the consciousness soul would be unable to develop; so it is essential for humanity to undergo this trial.

It is important to face up squarely to the whole situation, for if the negative side of evolution in the fifth post-Atlantean epoch were to develop alone, war and conflict would be unavoidable even in the most petty situations. So we see that certain requirements are beginning to arise instinctually of which we must become increasingly aware, and it is one of the tasks of spiritual science in the fifth post-Atlantean epoch to help human beings become more and more conscious of these.

I need only mention a single phrase to show how a remedy can be sought for this one direction that human development must necessarily take, a remedy for the difficulties we encounter in understanding one another. That phrase is: social understanding. Because we are living in the era of the consciousness soul we must generate more and more social understanding in this fifth post-Atlantean epoch. This one phrase sums up needs that did not yet exist to anything like the same extent in the fourth post-Atlantean epoch. Those who have studied the structure of Greek and Roman society know that individualism was not nearly as marked as it is now in European society or indeed in the society of America in the way it has been derived from Europe.

We can reach a clear understanding of this by comparing human beings with animal species. (Using a crass comparison is useful when trying to understand something.) Why do the animals of a species live amongst themselves within set limitations? It is because they are caused to do so by their group soul, by the soul of their species. This is inborn in the species, it is taken for granted by the animals; they remain within its confines and cannot grow beyond it. Human beings, however, must grow beyond their species. Every human being must develop individually. In particular today, in the era of the consciousness soul, this individual development is one of the main aspects of life. A hint of the group soul element still presided over the culture of Greece and Rome. We see there how people were situated within a social order that was quite strict, even though it was formed more by moral forces. In the fifth post-Atlantean epoch such orders will increasingly be dismantled. The hint of the group soul element that still existed in the fourth post-Atlantean epoch has become meaningless in the fifth. Its place must be taken by conscious social understanding, which means that whatever arises out of a deeper understanding of proper individual human nature must now be allowed to come to the fore.

It is spiritual science that will develop this proper understanding. When the circles who work with it begin to develop spiritual science away from the abstract and more and more towards real life, then a quite specific kind of knowledge about the human being and interest in the human being will begin to gain ground. There will be those who have a gift for teaching others about the different temperaments human beings have, and the different dispositions, about the way someone with a particular temperament must be treated in a certain way, while someone else, with another temperament combined with such and such a disposition, must be treated in a different way. Those with a talent for this will teach the others who need to learn something, showing them the different types of human being and how to treat one type in this way and another in that. Practical psychology, practical study of the human soul, will be cultivated, and also the practical study of life. These will lead to a real social understanding of human evolution.

What kind of social understanding has appeared on the scene so far? Up to now only abstract ideals have appeared, all kinds of abstract Utopias about how humanity and nations can be made happy—socialisms of one sort or another. If these social ideas were to be introduced in practice, we should soon see how not to do things. The fact is that there is no point in beginning by founding societies or sects with specific programmes. What needs to spread first of all is a true understanding of the human being, a practical knowledge of man, and specifically a knowledge that allows us to understand the growing child correctly and shows us how every child develops with his or her own individuality. Such an understanding would teach us how to lead our life in a way that enables us to develop appropriate durable relationships, those relationships that can become the most fruitful for life, when the right karmic effects rise up in us through meeting another person with whom we are to have a closer relationship of whatever kind.

What is needed today is a practical understanding of the human being, a truly practical interest in humanity. So far we have not made much progress in this. How do we judge people we meet today? By liking or disliking them. Look about you and you will see how in most cases this is the only judgement people make. Or if other judgements play a part as well, then these are entirely based on this one aspect of whether a person is likeable or not, or whether one likes this quality in him and dislikes that one. These are nothing but prejudices. We have a preconceived idea of what people ought to be like, and we make judgements about them if they do not fit in with this idea. We shall be unable to make progress in reaching a truly practical understanding of the human being unless we stop this way of liking or disliking on the basis of prejudice, on the basis of pet theories we have about one characteristic or another, and begin to take people for what they are.

When two people meet, whatever the circumstances, it happens so frequently that one of them immediately reacts with antipathy and dislikes the other one. Thereafter everything he or she does with regard to that person is tinged with this dislike. Very often a karmic relationship is completely extinguished by such behaviour, or it is sent off on an entirely wrong course and has to be postponed until the next incarnation when these two meet again. Sympathies and antipathies are the greatest enemies of genuine social interest, but very often little account is taken of this. If you know how important genuine social understanding is for the further evolution of humanity, you will be filled with dismay at the way some teachers behave in school when they show their prejudices in favour of one pupil and against another. This is often terrible, for the important thing is to accept the pupils as they are and make the very best of what is there.

Attitudes like this affect our social arrangements, such as our social laws that so frequently blot out the teacher's own individuality in a terrible way, preventing him from developing a real understanding of individuality. A true understanding of spiritual science must have the effect of inspiring a general interest in a practical understanding of the soul and of the human being. This is necessary so that social understanding can come about, social understanding as a counterbalance to the difficulties that are arising in mutual understanding between individuals.

It is this that must come to the fore in the fifth post-Atlantean epoch so that humanity as a whole can fully develop the consciousness soul. Human beings always have to undergo trials when such developments are under way, for they are resisted by the forces of opposition. So feelings of sympathy and antipathy will become widespread, and only in the conscious struggle against superficial likes and dislikes will the consciousness soul be rightly born.

Another obstacle to social understanding between one human being and another will be ever-increasing feelings of nationalism. In their present form these have only really become excessive since the nineteenth century, and they are thoroughly opposed to social understanding and to genuine interest between one human being and another. In the way these nationalistic confrontations, these national feelings of sympathy and antipathy are appearing, they are becoming a terrible trial for humanity, for they can only be healed by being overcome. If nationalistic sympathies and antipathies continue to prevail in the way they have begun, humanity will pass by the development of the consciousness soul in a dream. Nationalistic feelings are its very opposite, for they prevent human beings from becoming independent and turn them instead into nothing but a caricature of one national group or another.

This is the first matter we should take notice of if we want to look at the practical side of the otherwise abstract statement: that the consciousness soul must be particularly developed in the fifth post-Atlantean epoch.

Something else can also not be avoided during this fifth post-Atlantean epoch if the consciousness soul is to unfold properly. In so far as they become ever more individual, people will find that religious life will grow increasingly barren if it does not adapt to the fifth post-Atlantean epoch but remains in a form that was suitable for the fourth epoch. Since people then tended to be more comfortable in groups, group religions were what was needed. Common dogmas, common religious principles and thoughts had to be imposed, as it were, by authority on groups of people. But since the urge to be individual will grow ever stronger during the fifth post-Atlantean epoch, the group religions will no longer touch hearts and the individuality of souls. People will simply not understand what the group religions are trying to tell them.

During the fourth post-Atlantean epoch it was still possible to teach human beings about Christ in a manner suitable for groups, but in the fifth epoch Christ is actually already entering into individual souls. Unconsciously or subconsciously we all bear Christ within us now, and we shall have to learn to understand him once more within ourselves. This cannot happen if fixed, rigid dogmas are imposed on us, but we can work towards it by trying hard to do everything possible to make Christ comprehensible to human beings in every way, and by promoting religious understanding in all its many facets. To this end an ever greater tolerance must be practised with regard to the thoughts of religious life during this fifth post-Atlantean epoch. In the fourth epoch those who worked for religion did so by passing on to their contemporaries a certain number of dogmas and fixed principles, but in the fifth epoch this must change entirely. Something quite different is necessary.

Since people are now growing ever more individual, one must try and extricate oneself from anything dogmatic and describe what one is able to pass on to others out of one's personal inner experience in such a way that their own free life of religious thought can develop within them.

In the fifth post-Atlantean epoch the dogmatic religions, the fixed dogmatic confessions will actually kill religious life. Therefore in this fifth epoch the right way to begin is to help people understand how things done in a certain way in the early Christian centuries were appropriate for their time but that subsequent centuries need something different. And there are also other religions. One attempts to make the essence of other religions comprehensible, and one attempts to bring about understanding of the various ways in which Christ can be regarded. In this way we can bring to every soul what that soul needs for its own deepening. We do not try to mould that soul, for we let its own freedom of thought unfold, especially in the realm of religion.

Just as social understanding is necessary on the one hand, as I have described in connection with the fifth post-Atlantean epoch, so is freedom of thought in the realm of religion also essential for the development of the consciousness soul, social understanding in the realm of human relationships, and freedom of thought in the realm of religion.

The attempt we are making to enter into religious life with more and more understanding, so that we can comprehend our fellow human beings even when each unfolds his own religious life, must be taken more and more seriously, for it is a fundamental necessity for the fifth post-Atlantean epoch. Human beings must achieve it consciously through their own effort.

In the era of the consciousness soul, especially, ahrimanic powers are attacking this freedom of thought most violently.[4] An example of this is the way the confessions everywhere are inimical to one of the fundamental aspects of spiritual science—the spread of freedom of thought. We see how often the science of the spirit is slandered simply because it wants to consider the birth of the consciousness soul with full and illumined understanding and does not want to spread the kind of religious life that was appropriate for the intellectual or mind soul in the fourth post-Atlantean epoch. The forms in which Christianity is cast were created in the fourth post-Atlantean epoch out of the needs of Graeco-Roman culture. As ecclesiastical forms today they are already inappropriate, and they will become increasingly more inappropriate with regard to the growth of freedom of thought, which must more and more come to the fore.

At the very moment when the first seeds of the need for freedom of thought began to quicken, the opposing powers also began to act in what might be called the Jesuitism of the various religions (although this definition includes much that really ought to be described in more detail). This was called into being specifically in order to provide the strongest opposition against the freedom of thought that is essential for the life of the fifth post-Atlantean epoch. For the development of this epoch it will become increasingly urgent to eliminate in every field this Jesuitism that has been set against the freedom of thought; for freedom of thought, raying out from religious life, must unfold more and more in every realm. Because freedom of thought has to be acquired independently by every individual, humanity is placed in this situation of having to contend with a trial, and the greatest difficulties are arising everywhere. These difficulties are all the greater the more people find developing clarity of consciousness a nuisance. Instead, they delude themselves about it, although it is the very thing they ought to be developing in the fifth post-Atlantean epoch.

We are witnessing a pitched battle between incipient freedom of thought and the power of authority, which has been handed on to us from past times. The desire to delude ourselves about our belief in authority is very strong; our faith in authority has increased enormously, and under its influence we are becoming helpless about making up our own mind. In the fourth post-Atlantean epoch people were born with a natural gift of good sense, but now we have to acquire and develop this good sense ourselves. Belief in authority is preventing this, for we are entirely taken over by this blind belief. Look at the animal kingdom and see how helpless we appear in comparison with animals, who have no intellect. Animals have instincts that guide them in ways that are good for them, even leading them back to health when they fall ill. Human beings, on the other hand, are working against an ability to form judgements about what to do in such circumstances. Instead, they defer to authority.

It is not easy, for example, for people to form their own opinions about how to lead a healthy life. There are of course all kinds of groups and societies making praiseworthy attempts at this, but such efforts must become much, much stronger. Above all we must understand that our tendency to have faith in authority is on the increase, and that whole theories are being elaborated to back up convictions that strengthen this faith in authority even more.

In the field of medicine, in the law, but also in all other fields, people are declaring themselves incapable of acquiring their own knowledge and are instead accepting whatever science tells them. This is of course understandable in view of modern life's complicated nature. People are growing ever more helpless in face of authority, and it is the main principle of Jesuitism systematically to strengthen this faith in authority. The Jesuitism of the Catholic religion is only a special application amongst many other applications in other fields that are, however, not so easily noticed.

Jesuitism began with the dogmatic Jesuitism of the Church with its purpose of letting the power of the Pope—which originated in the fourth post-Atlantean epoch—continue on into the fifth post-Atlantean epoch, in which it is no longer appropriate. But this Jesuitical principle will gradually come to be applied in other realms of life as well. There is already a form of Jesuitism in the medical profession that is barely distinguishable from the Jesuitism in dogmatic religion. We can observe how medical dogmatism is tending to enhance the power of the medical profession. This is the nature of Jesuitism in other fields as well, and it will grow stronger and stronger.

Human beings will become increasingly constrained by whatever higher authorities impose on them, and the salvation of the fifth post-Atlantean epoch will lie in countering the

132 THE MEANING OF LIFE

ahrimanic opposition facing us and asserting the rights of the consciousness soul as it strives to develop. But this can only come about if human beings—since they are no longer born with a ready-made common sense in the way they are with two ready-made arms—can truly strive to develop their common sense, their capacity to form sound judgements. The development of the consciousness soul requires freedom of thought, but this freedom of thought can only flourish in a specific kind of atmosphere.

I have been directing your attention to the difficulties that exist in the fifth post-Atlantean epoch which is striving specifically to develop the consciousness soul. But this consciousness soul, precisely because it is the consciousness soul, has to come up against resistance and experience trials. Thus both social understanding and freedom of thought are encountering the strongest obstacles. Yet people do not even realize that these obstacles exist, for in the wisest circles they are regarded as the best thing, to be built up further rather than opposed.

Nonetheless, there are very many people who do have an open heart and a good understanding of the situation facing modern human beings. They understand very well the way karmic relationships are driving people into the crises mentioned earlier in which children can no longer understand their parents, nor parents their children, and in which neither brothers and sisters nor nations and peoples can get on together any longer. There are already plenty of people who watch with a bleeding heart these situations which, though necessary, can only work properly if they are rightly understood. Motivation for a new way of working in the world must be wrung consciously from the heart's blood. The estrangement of individuals from one another will happen of its own accord, but what is to flow from the human heart must be consciously sought. Every individual soul faces difficulties in the fifth post-Atlantean epoch, for only in overcoming these difficulties will those trials come about through which the consciousness soul can be developed.

Many people today say that they have no sense for what they should be making of themselves, or that they do not know how to set out in life in the right way. This is because they have not yet found the right way of thinking clearly about the needs of the present time or about their individual situation. In many cases such an impasse results in physical illness or physical instability. We must seek ever more intensively for a right understanding of this. Humanity in the fifth post-Atlantean epoch will of necessity find itself beset by the distress of soul described just now. Many people see this as I have described it, and feel the necessity for social understanding on the one hand and freedom of thought on the other; but very, very few are inclined to turn to the right means of help. This is because so often all kinds of idealistic sounding phrases are used in attempts to describe what is necessary for social understanding.

Such a lot is written nowadays about the need to treat growing youngsters individually, with all kinds of detailed theories being thought up in every possible educational field. Yet this is not what is really needed. What should be disseminated in an understanding way are as many positive descriptions as possible of how human beings really develop, positive descriptions in the sense of being like a 'natural history' of individual human development. Wherever we can, we should recount how person A—or person B or person C—has actually developed, by entering lovingly into the way a specific human being we have right here in front of us is growing up. Descriptions like this are needed more than anything else. We need studies of real life, the will to understand life, not to elaborate programmes, for a programme based on theories is an enemy of the fifth post-Atlantean epoch.

In the fifth post-Atlantean epoch of culture it would be appropriate for societies to form in such a way that the individual human beings belonging to them are seen as the main element. In their fellowship together these people would achieve truly individual results. Yet what actually happens today? Statutes are drawn up. These are all well and good, and indeed perhaps necessary since outer circumstances require such things. But in our field in particular we should be fully aware that any talk of programmes and statutes is nothing but a concession to existing circumstances. The important thing must be the way individuals live together and what results from this; mutual understanding is what matters.

Many centuries of the fifth post-Atlantean epoch still lie ahead of us, so there will be opportunities for insight into the way individuals actually develop in real life to spread beyond the circles of those who already understand this and become general knowledge. But for the moment the only idea people have is to impose the torture of paragraphs and regulations on everything. High-minded discourses resound from every pulpit and platform purporting to be concerned with life. Yet the ideas and ideals put forward in these discourses are positively drenched in abstractions. This cannot be what is needed, for the real matter in hand is to penetrate into real life, into what actually happens in life, in an understanding way. So how can this be done?

It goes without saying that entirely reasonable objections can be raised about what I have been saying. 'How,' people will ask, 'can we learn to form judgements about all the statements made today by various authorities? Think what you have to learn to become a physician! Obviously a physician has to learn these things, but we cannot learn them as well, and in addition everything a lawyer has to learn, or someone who wants to become an artist!'

It goes without saying that it would be impossible to do this. But it is not a matter of becoming creative in these fields, but of learning how to form judgements. We must be able to let those in authority do their work, but at the same time we must become capable of forming judgements about them. We cannot learn to do this by thoroughly studying every branch of specialist knowledge, but what we can do is acquire the possibility of forming judgements through something that will shape our understanding and our capacity to judge. This something is not the material knowledge of the various specialisms; it is all-embracing knowledge of the spirit.

Spiritual science must become the central kind of knowledge. Spiritual science will not only inform us about all that is involved in human evolution; by the very kind of thinking it cultivates it will also develop in us a sound power of understanding. Such a power has to be drawn up to the surface from greater depths today than was the case in the Graeco-Roman times of the fourth post-Atlantean epoch of culture. The way spiritual science forms concepts and develops inner pictures differs from the way other sciences work. Rather than enabling us to become an authority in any particular field, it teaches us how to form judgements. The reason for this will come to be understood little by little. There are mysterious powers in the human soul, and these secret, mystery powers will link the human soul with the spiritual world. Through this link that forms between the human soul and the spiritual world in consequence of our work in spiritual science we shall become capable of forming judgements when confronted by an authority in a particular instance. We shall not know what that authority can know, but when the authority acts on the basis of its knowledge in a specific case we shall be in a position to form a judgement about this action.

We should emphasize this strongly as something that must be brought about by spiritual science. Spiritual science does not merely instruct us; it helps us to become capable of forming judgements, it gives us the possibility of freedom of thought, of becoming independent in our thinking. Spiritual science does not turn us into physicians, but if we enter into it rightly it gives us the ability to judge what physicians do in public life. A thorough understanding of this point will give us much insight into forces that bring healing in the fifth post-Atlantean epoch. A tremendous amount is contained in the statement that spiritual science will alter the way human beings understand things, so that as a result they will become capable of forming judgements and achieving real freedom of thought through bringing powers of understanding to birth from the depths of their soul life. Only then will they truly acquire freedom of thought.

If I may now speak more in pictures, I would like to express this thought to you in a pictorial, imaginative form. Spiritual science tells us about the real spiritual world, the actual spiritual world, about elemental beings all around us, about hierarchies, angels, archangels and so on. We discover that the world is populated by actual spiritual content, spiritual powers and spiritual beings. Our knowing about those spiritual beings living in the spiritual world is not a matter of indifference to them. They were more or less indifferent about it during the fourth post-Atlantean epoch, but this is no longer the case in the fifth epoch. For human beings not to know about them is like depriving them of spiritual nourishment. The spiritual world is most certainly linked to the physical world here on the earth. You will perhaps understand this better if I tell you something that may for the moment appear paradoxical although it is absolutely true. Perhaps one cannot say too much as yet, but some truths need to be expressed so that human beings do not have to live without them.

Here on earth we are correct in saying that Christ entered earthly life—in which he has since been present—through the Mystery of Golgotha. From one point of view it can be felt as a source of happiness that Christ has entered into earthly life. But put yourself in the situation of the angels, a situation that is not my invention but one that every genuine spiritual researcher will discover to be true. From the angels' point of view the opposite was experienced in the spiritual world. In order to come to human beings, Christ has departed from the angels' sphere. From their point of view they have to say that Christ went away from them through the Mystery of Golgotha. They have as much justification for being sad as human beings have for being glad that Christ has come to them while they dwell in a physical body.

These are real thoughts, and those who know the spiritual world know that only one salvation is possible for the angels, and that this involves what I have just been saying. It is that human beings on the earth in their physical body so live with the thought of Christ that since the Mystery of Golgotha this thought of Christ can shine up to the angels like a light. Human beings can say that Christ has entered into them and that they can develop in a way that will allow him to remain in them: 'Not I, but Christ in me.' Angels, on the other hand, have to say that Christ departed from their sphere, that in the Christ-filled thoughts of individual human beings he shines up to them like so many stars. Since the Mystery of Golgotha they find him again in what shines up to them like this. It is a real relationship between the spiritual world and the human world.

Another expression of this relationship is the way the

spiritual beings living in the spiritual world outside us look with pleasure, with joy and satisfaction, upon the thoughts we have about their world. They can only come to our assistance if we can think about them, even if we have not yet reached the point of being able to look into the spiritual world clairvoyantly. They can help us if we know about them. Help reaches us from the spiritual world in return for our study of spiritual knowledge. Not merely the things we learn about, the knowledge itself, but also the beings of higher hierarchies themselves come to our assistance if we know about them.

As we continue to be confronted by authorities in the fifth post-Atlantean epoch, it will be good to be backed up not only by our own human understanding but also by what the spiritual beings manage to bring about in our understanding through the fact that we know of them. They make us capable of judging what comes from authority. The spiritual world helps us. We need it, we must know about it, we must take it into our conscious understanding. This is the third thing that must come about for the fifth post-Atlanean epoch of culture.

The first is a social understanding of human beings, the second is to achieve freedom of thought, the third is to attain a living knowledge of the spiritual world through spiritual science. These three must be the great and real ideals of the fifth post-Atlantean epoch. In social life, social understanding must arise. In religious life and in the way human souls live with one another, freedom of thought must come about. In the realm of knowledge, recognition and understanding of the spirit must come into being. These are the three great aims and incentives of the fifth epoch. We must develop in the light of these three, for they are the right torches for our time.

Many people *feel* strongly that there is a need for a new kind of community life nowadays, and that new concepts must be developed. Yet the ultimate conclusions to be drawn from this feeling fail to be grasped either by their good will or their power of understanding. This is demonstrated by the attitude many individuals have towards the endeavours of spiritual science or anthroposophy. We can disregard the malicious slanders that are expressed against spiritual science, or against theosophy or anthroposophy, and the hostile attitudes that arise for one reason or another. But look instead at the honest good will that exists in many, many people whose aim it is to create incentives in humanity that move in the same direction as those of the fifth post-Atlantean epoch.

Think of the many reformers who are appearing in all kinds of fields, of the many socially-minded clergymen, and of other preachers on social matters emerging from non-theological, non-religious circles. They have the very best intentions, and are leading people towards aims that are entirely compatible with the life of our time. Very much good will exists, so let us look for a moment at what this good will comprises and not at the ill will that is also there. So long as the good will remains in the realm of generalizations, however warm the feelings by which it is sustained, it cannot help us unless knowledge can also come to life, knowledge given only by spiritual science about the achievement of the three great goals: social understanding (based on understanding the human being), freedom of thought, and knowledge of the spirit. At present, however, people have not even reached the beginning of this knowledge, except for that small group gathered together around the world view of spiritual science.

There are, though, some pleasing and generous developments in this direction, of which I should like to give you an example that came to my notice 'by accident', as they say, although in reality it was through karma. I happened to notice a small book in a shop window, and I bought it because of the impression the title made on me.[5] It describes the modern human being, his aims, and what influences him as he grows up. The book tells of the many things in the external world that help people and make their life more comfortable and easy, and the pleasures that are derived from new inventions such as steam power and electricity. Then it goes on more tellingly to stress something by saying that while the pace of living has greatly increased, life has also become more rich. These things are emphasized with enthusiasm; the marvellous cultural achievements of modern times are described, and it is pointed out how much more fortunate people are today than they were in the days when life was duller, sadder and more at the mercy of the inevitable. The book then correctly describes what I pointed out earlier as the difficulties of the fifth post-Atlantean epoch. But there is no recognition of the fact that these are actually the consequence of this fifth post-Atlantean epoch and its requirement of developing the consciousness soul. The author fails to see clearly what is going on, and this is the point I am trying to make. He is open-hearted and full of feeling when he says: 'It may be noted that in describing the inner path along which our time has developed we took our departure from the joys of life and the pleasures of existence. Yet we have to conclude this chapter by describing the profound inner distress of soul now prevalent. What we are experiencing here on a small scale is being experienced by the present age on a grand scale.' (By 'small scale' he is referring to the place where he happens to be living at the moment.) 'Our culture is incomparably more abundant, and our life more energetic and beautiful than at almost any other period in history; and yet a profound distress of soul is beginning to envelop whole swathes of the population.'

Having rightly recognized the symptoms, the author goes on to describe various remedies for overcoming this helpless distress and for finding incentives that can guide modern humanity in the right direction. Amongst these he cites what he calls 'theosophy', and tells us how he got to know it. Amongst so many who are antagonistic to theosophy, here is one who feels kindly towards it and has the best will in the world to get to know it, someone who has made a study of it and whom we should therefore take seriously.[6] I am not telling you this for frivolous reasons, but because it is most important that we should concern ourselves with the positive resonance our spiritual science is experiencing in the life around us.

Having discussed how mysticism that does not become 'mystical' wants to bring about the deepening of life and assuage the distress of soul, the author continues: 'Beside mysticism we have theosophy. Many people regard it as something that merely aims to provide surrogates in place of proven strengths; or else they see it only as an inclination to syncretism and eclecticism.' He means a combination of all kinds of religious creeds and world views. As you know, some of those who do not go more deeply into spiritual science talk of it as though it were warmed-up Gnosticism, and so on. But this author goes a step further, for he talks of those who 'see it only as an inclination to syncretism and eclecticism to suit individual tendencies, and who lump it together with some of the less enlightened concomitants of present-day life, such as superstition, spiritualism, ghost-watching, symbolism and similar expressions of intellectual pursuits that titillate by their mysteriousness. But it is not like this. One does this movement an injustice if one fails to recognize the profound inner values and references that come to expression in it.' You can see that this man is kindly disposed towards us. He continues: 'Instead we should regard it—or at least the circle around Steiner—as a religious movement amongst our contemporaries which, although not original but only syncretic, directs its attention towards the foundations of life.' Let us hope that, with all his good will, this man will one day also discover its originality!

'We may judge it as a movement that wants to satisfy people's interest in the supersensible and which therefore wants to grow beyond a realism that remains trapped in what is sense-perceptible. Above all we may regard it as a movement that draws people's attention towards a personal consideration of the moral dilemmas they are facing, and a movement that aims to work towards an inner rebirth through scrupulous attention to self-development...' As I said before, I am not reading this to you for frivolous reasons but because, given what is otherwise said about anthroposophy, it is rather relevant to learn about opinions such as those expressed here.

'One need only read Steiner's introductory book on theosophy in order to discover the earnestness with which the human being is here exhorted to work at his moral refinement and self-improvement. In its speculations with regard to the supersensible, theosophy is furthermore a reaction against materialism, although,' (please take special notice of what now follows) 'in this respect, it easily departs from the firm ground of facts, going too far off course into hypotheses, into clairvoyant fantasies, into a realm of dreams, so that it retains too little force for the realities involved in shaping individual and social life. Nevertheless, we will and must register theosophy as a corrective influence in the cultural processes of the present time.'

The only thing that really displeases this man is the matter of ascending to knowledge of the spirit, to concrete, realistic knowledge of the spirit. He wants what, in his opinion too, can arise out of the theosophy by way of incentives for the refinement of the human being, but as yet he fails to realize that now, in the fifth post-Atlantean epoch, this can only come through a real, concrete knowledge of the spirit. He does not recognize the roots. He wants the fruits without the roots. He does not see the overall picture. It is most interesting to consider this man, for as we have seen he has studied my book *Theosophy* with enthusiasm and yet cannot understand that the one does not exist without the other.[7] He wants to cut off this book's head while retaining the body, for he regards the body as something of value.

This relates directly to what I was saying just now when I pointed out that social understanding and freedom of thought were necessary. People can understand this, but they cannot yet recognize that the third element, knowledge of the spirit, must form the basis for our fifth post-Atlantean epoch. One of the most important tasks of spiritual science and its stream is to open people's eyes to this. The ascent to spiritual worlds is still described by many as a fantasy. They fail to recognize that the loss of knowledge of the spiritual worlds is the very thing that has brought about materialism with its concomitant lack of social understanding, as well as today's materialistic life and materialistic attitudes. In order to find out why it is still so difficult for people to recognize the necessary existence of real spiritual worlds, we should look in particular at those who are otherwise favourably disposed towards us. We must increase our efforts to win understanding for the impulses I have been speaking about in today's lecture.

The booklet I have been quoting from is entitled 'Concepts entertained by educated people'. As I said, I found it 'accidentally', for it was published two years ago. It reproduces a lecture given in Hamburg by Professor Dr Friedrich Mahling during the 37th Congress of the Internal Mission Society on 23 September 1913. I am rather surprised that no one amongst our circle has mentioned this book, for surely someone must have seen it between 1914 and now? It really is important to follow up the various threads that interweave between all kinds of areas. It is important to take notice of the vulgar abuse and mockery, which is much more prevalent, but also of instances where honest attempts are being made to understand us, as in the present case. These can teach us about the real difficulties even people with the most honest attitude are still experiencing.

My lecture today was aimed at showing what are to be the three great ideals, the concrete ideals for the fifth post-Atlantean epoch: social, genuine understanding of the human being, freedom of thought, spiritual knowledge. These three ideals must in future act as guides for the sciences. They must ennoble and purify life, they must give incentives to morality, and for modern humanity as a whole they must pervade and direct all aspects of life in the most comprehensive way. However, the first two—social understanding and freedom of thought—will remain unfulfilled unless knowledge of the spirit can join them, for it is the consciousness soul that must be developed. As its highest stage the consciousness soul possesses the spirit-self, which must be prepared in the sixth post-Atlantean epoch of culture. This cannot be developed if preparations are not made through the inner independence of the human being that is achieved by unfolding the consciousness soul.

In our work with spiritual science we must take into account that what we see as abstract truths definitely have within them a magical power that need only be set free for the brightest light to be shed on all of life. Wherever individuals find themselves in life, in whatever field of science or field of practical work, even the most lowly, they will be sharing in the great tasks of our time if they are rightly able to bring to life for their own field the things we take up as abstract truths during our meetings. Real joy will enter such souls, as opposed to superficial cheerfulness, real joy is linked to a seriousness which sustains our lives, gives us strength and allows us not merely to enjoy life but to become real workers for life.

In this sense these three concrete ideals for social life and knowledge will also enable the consciousness soul in this fifth post-Atlantean epoch to understand the Mystery of Golgotha in a new way, and to accept the Christ. For we must forge real links with the spiritual worlds; we must find out how these worlds, too, relate to the Christ-impulse, to this central incentive of Earth evolution. This is what the Christ-impulse will become for us under the influence of the thoughts that come into earthly existence from the spiritual world. For since the Mystery of Golgotha thoughts can light up in human souls on earth, thoughts like bright stars that bring comfort, as I described, even to the world of the angels, who have lost Christ in their sphere but can see him shining towards them from the sphere of human thinking.

Spiritual knowledge should most certainly not be described as a fantasy. Spiritual knowledge strives to find real ways of alleviating the distress of soul that is necessarily linked with the fifth post-Atlantean epoch.

This is what I wanted to speak about today. I do hope we shall meet here again before too long, and until then I hope we can remain together in our thoughts and continue to work on in the spirit of our movement.[8]

7. How to Listen to the Spirit[1]

We are living at a time when the aim towards which anthroposophical spiritual science has been striving for many years has become much more obvious. It would therefore be rather satisfying if those involved in this movement could become convinced heart and soul that the fiery signs of our times are indeed proof of its being urgently needed. For whether events in the external world are stormy or not, and whatever it is that is striving to emerge from profound depths of human evolution, the essential nature of what is happening today can only be grasped by studying events that are imperceptible to those ordinary human powers of perception still usual amongst us today, events which only a spiritual viewpoint can reveal.

I should like to begin by mentioning one such phenomenon that almost escapes notice amongst the many stormy events of today. It is regarded as something insignificant, but its importance is known to those who from spiritual sources have acquired the ability to study life as it really is.

It may sound extraordinary, but the fact is that for the last seven or eight, or ten, years those who are able to study life as it really is have been observing quite a different expression on the faces of new-born babies. This is going unnoticed on the whole, for the most important things in life pass unheeded nowadays. But those who have acquired an eye for such things know that the many children born during the last seven to ten years wear a melancholy expression. They appear to be holding back from the world. From the earliest days of life, from the first weeks onwards, something different can be seen in children's physiognomy. If we investigate this remarkable fact, which people find so peculiar, we discover that the souls entering the world through birth bear something within them, from before conception and birth, that gives them this melancholy expression. Hidden though it often is behind all their smiles, it is nevertheless there in the faces of these children, almost from birth. Formerly children did not wear this expression. In their souls—quite unconsciously, of course— they have a mood of reluctance about entering into life. For almost ten years now, souls going through the process of birth have been experiencing a kind of hindrance, a barrier to entering the physical world.

Before entering the physical world through conception and birth, the human being has an important experience in the spiritual world the effects of which ray out into his coming life and are active in it. Here on earth we die, we pass through the gate of death, laying aside our physical body and taking our soul into the spiritual world; it still bears within it the effects of all it has experienced in the physical world. Having passed through the gate of death, our soul on the whole resembles whatever it has directly experienced here in earthly life. When they have passed through the gate of death, these souls encounter other souls who are preparing to descend into physical bodies in the near future. (This is a fact. I can only inform you of it, for these things can only be brought from the spiritual world through actual experience of them.) This meeting between the souls who have just passed through the gate of death and those who are about to enter the physical world through the gate of birth is an important event. Its effect is decisive in many respects. Its purpose is to inoculate the descending souls with some kind of idea of what awaits them here. This meeting is the source of the impulse that impresses such a peculiar expression of melancholy on the faces of children entering the world today. They do not want to enter the world of which they have learnt through this meeting, for they know that in a sense their 'spiritual plumage' will be very much ruffled by what humanity, immersed in materialistic attitudes, materialistic views and materialistic actions, is experiencing on the earth today. Together with other things, this event—which, naturally, can only be confirmed spiritually—casts a strong light over the whole of our time. Present times can only be understood on such a basis, and we ought to strive for this understanding.

I have begun with something that can, of course, only be apprehended through spiritual perception. But other events in our time speak to us loudly and clearly and can be obvious to anyone who, even if lacking spiritual vision, does not go through life half asleep. We have watched as the great calamity of the World War spread across the globe over the last four or five years, causing untold harm. Again and again we turn our thoughts to the outward and visible causes of this terrible calamity for humanity—as, I believe, every wide-awake soul must do. We study the course of this calamity and, finally, the events that have followed from it over large areas of the globe. It seems to me that one thing must be obvious to every soul who is really awake. Consider the peculiar fact that this calamity of the World War burst over Central Europe without anyone actually knowing how it came about. People ask how it could have happened, pronounce one person or another guilty, and then—when they imagine they have pin-pointed the guilty party—repeat again and again: 'Surely this cannot be what happened; there must have been some other factor at work.'

People tell themselves that a great social unrest has developed out of the calamity of the World War. Whether they belong to a party or not, people try to understand what ought to be done in today's troubled social situation. Yet all the thoughts they arrive at are only 'thought-mummies' in the face of current events—thoughts that are powerless before the impetus of events and quite inadequate in face of their true character. If we look more closely at all this, especially now when all kinds of memoirs are being published by persons who appeared to be directly concerned in the outbreak of the world calamity, we have to ask ourselves: 'Were these people genuinely involved in the events of four or five years ago? Did they really know what they were doing? Had they the remotest conception as to the far-reaching consequences of what their intellects had concocted?' People ought more and more to admit to themselves today what the Russian minister Sukhomlinov admitted in court.[2] Speaking of the three or four hours in which he had had to make his most important decisions, he said: 'I must have lost my reason then; I must have been mad!'

Such things are profoundly significant. They point to the widespread mental confusion existing amongst the individuals concerned at that moment. Those who are properly able to comprehend the terrible nature of present world events will realize what people will more and more come to see, that there was not so very much moral failure but all the more intellectual blundering through sheer incapacity to grasp world events.

Things are no different today. How helpless, in the main, is the great majority of people in the face of the world events that have come upon them. This ought to raise the most serious question as to what is really behind it all. The answer is extremely difficult for our materialistically minded age to grasp. It is that precisely from the moment in history when the waves of materialism are rising higher than ever the strongest spiritual force that has ever willed to enter human life from the spiritual world is now seeking to enter.

This is what characterizes our time. Since the beginning of

the final third of the nineteenth century the spirit, the spiritual world, wills to reveal itself to human beings with all its might. Yet human beings have gradually reached the point in their evolution when they want to use only their physical body as the instrument by which they receive anything at all in the world. Their materialistic outlook has accustomed them to establish the theory that the physical brain is the tool of thinking, of feeling also, and even of will. They have not drawn this conclusion without good reason, for human evolution has indeed gradually reached the point when only the physical body can be used as the tool for mental activity.

This is why we find ourselves today at that infinitely important juncture in human evolution when on the one hand the spiritual world wills to reveal itself with immense power, while on the other hand human beings must find the strength to extricate themselves from their greatest entanglement in the material world and receive anew the revelations of the spirit.

Human beings today confront the greatest test of strength, the test of their ability to work in freedom towards the spirit which approaches them of its own accord, if they do not shut themselves off from it. The spirit can no longer reveal itself to human beings through all kinds of subconscious and unconscious processes. It is time for human beings to receive the light of the spirit through a free, inner deed. All the confusion and want of clarity in which people live today results from the fact that they must receive something that they do not yet want to receive—an entirely new understanding of things.

The old ways of thinking, the old ways of regarding world events have come to full expression in the frightful, horrific calamity of the World War. The infinitely significant warning signs are nothing other than a call to remodel our ways of thinking, to try a new way of looking at the world, for the old way can only lead again and again to chaos and confusion. It is time we realized this. It is time to realize that in 1914 the leading statesmen had reached the point at which nothing more could be achieved with the old modes of thinking. As a result they led humanity into misfortune. People must impress this fact strongly upon themselves, or they will not form a strong resolution really to meet the spirit and the life of the spirit in freedom and inwardness of soul.

The tragic thing about the present time is that we see things being revealed everywhere that are incomprehensible when approached from previous points of view and previous conceptions of life. Yet people cling firmly to those old points of view and conceptions of life and simply do not want to come to new modes of understanding. The anthroposophical view of the world wants to prepare humanity for such new modes. On the whole its only opponent has been people's inner inertia and sluggishness of soul that prevents them from rousing themselves to bring the inner forces of their soul to meet the spiritual wave breaking in on our life so powerfully today.

As I have just said, people are no longer in the habit of using anything but their physical body for thinking, and the ultimate consequence of this is the materialistic view of the world. There is one aspect, though, that simply must be understood today. Whereas nature as studied by science, with all its many triumphs, can indeed be comprehended through the instrument of the physical brain, this instrument is no use at all for understanding human life. We can only understand human life if we can rise to a thinking that is not produced by the physical body alone. This is the kind of thinking that should be cultivated by the anthroposophical world view. Of course people say they do not understand the anthroposophical outlook—in the way it is given in books or presented in lectures, and we can quite believe them. But what do they mean when they say they do not understand? They simply mean that they want to use their physical brain for understanding, rather than learning another kind of thinking that does not seek the prop of the physical brain. Obviously they cannot understand the anthroposophical view of the world by means of the type of thinking they prefer. It is not that you have to be clairvoyant, but you must practise a kind of thinking that is not bound to the physical brain. Healthy common sense is not bound to the brain, for it is only sick, materialistic common sense that is brain-bound. By applying healthy common sense to anthroposophical literature you train your thinking, your feeling and your will to become thinking, feeling and will that are appropriate for the events of the present time. The fact is that what the present requires of us cannot be grasped by the instrument of the physical body; it has to be grasped by the instrument of the etheric body, that body of formative forces that underlies the physical body.

The spiritual world that is striving to reveal itself to human beings is only making itself noticeable in their deeply unconscious feelings. People have a desperate fear of it. When they say they do not understand spiritual science, this is really only an excuse. The truth is that they are afraid of the spiritual world revealing itself. It is only because they do not want to admit this fear that people say they cannot understand spiritual science, or that it is not logical, or they choose some other excuse. The truth is that they are afraid, so they seek any kind of excuse in order to wriggle out of facing up to the really great problems. People are so relieved to escape from the great tasks and enigmas of our present time, for talk about the really important problems, from whatever point of view, makes them feel uncomfortable. So if they see such problems dealt with in one of Ibsen's plays they avoid taking them seriously by regarding this as 'merely' art.[3] Direct talk of the spiritual world penetrating the physical is uncomfortable. Björnson, too, has brought such things into his plays, but there is no need to 'believe' in such things, for they are 'merely' art.[4] People have an unconquerable fear of taking these things seriously.

Or again, take class conflict and the way the gulf between the governing and the proletarian classes has grown ever wider. The social question is full of enigmas. To speak about these enigmas is uncomfortable, but if you go and see Hauptmann's play *Die Weber* in the theatre there is no need to take a serious stand regarding the problems it presents;[5] you can enjoy having your emotions stirred up a little by the abysmal depths in human life, but there is no need to take it seriously for it is 'merely' art. People escape into something they need not take seriously.

This is a characteristic psychological phenomenon of our time. What lies behind it? Behind it lies the fact that in order to accord with the will of the spiritual world to reveal itself people ought to have been striving to take certain things seriously that cannot be comprehended via the instrument of the physical body, things that can only be comprehended through the power of Imagination, just as art itself can only be understood via Imagination.[6] The human physical body is constructed like a product of nature; the human etheric body is constructed like a work of art, like a real sculpture, except that it is in perpetual movement. What we receive for our enjoyment through understanding art must be intensified and illuminated; it must become actual perception: Imagination, Inspiration, Intuition. If it does, we shall understand what wants to reveal itself to us today, for what can only be understood spiritually is waiting expectantly behind the cover of today's events.

We ought to feel deeply that the spiritual revelation trying to enter into today's world can only be comprehended by spiritual science itself, which means by that thinking and feeling and by those inner motivations of will that can be trained by spiritual science and that belong in the same region as artistic perceptions—although these are not taken seriously and remain mere mirror images.

There have been occasions when I tried to draw attention to something that is urgently needed by the present time. Because of the philistine character of today's science, that monster of official academic science, it was of course not understood. In my book *The Philosophy of Freedom*, published in 1894, I gave one of the chapters the title 'Moral Imagination'.[7] In terms of spiritual science one might also say 'moral impulses of the imagination'. By doing this I wanted to point out that the domain usually reached only in artistic fantasy must now be taken seriously by human beings because it represents the level they will have to reach in order to receive the supersensible, which cannot be grasped by the brain. At the beginning of the 1890s I wanted to point out, at least with reference to morality, that it was time to take the spiritual element seriously.

We must begin to sense these things today. We must begin to sense that the thoughts and inner motivations being brought into the world right up to the calamity of the World War, and into these times of social upheaval, are no use any longer, and that we need new impulses. If you bring in a new impulse today, it tends to be the very last thing people are likely to understand. A living motivation is brought down directly from the spiritual world so that it can be a remedy for the evils of our time, yet what you hear is a chorus of squeals from all sides, from the extreme left to the extreme right, to the effect that it is all incomprehensible. Of course it is incomprehensible so long as the old forms of thinking are retained. Instead of remaining stuck in the old forms of thought, we must transform and remodel our whole soul.

Every external revolution today, no matter how agreeable to whichever party or class, will only lead us down the worst of blind alleys, and inflict the most terrible misery on humanity, unless it is illumined by an inner revolution of the soul. This involves abandoning one's absorption in purely materialistic views and preparing to receive the spiritual wave that wants to pour into human evolution as a new revelation. The revolution from matter to spirit is the only salutary revolution. All the others are merely the childhood diseases—like scarlet fever or measles—afflicting the forerunner of what is trying to come to birth in a healthy way in the emergence of the spirit at the present time.

We need to form a strong inner resolution in order to be equal to the demands our present time is making on us. We have to consider in all earnestness that it is a spiritual world that is trying to break in on our life, and that spiritual forces are now here upon which we should make all our decisions, our deeds, our whole thinking dependent. We are required to do this now. Many changes are coming about in our time, and I should like to point out one of the symptoms which may sound strange when spoken of, but which is of the utmost importance when viewed spiritually.

I have just spoken to you of the etheric body as a necessary instrument for a degree of spiritual understanding about something that in art need only be shown as a reflection. From spiritual science we know that in addition to our physical body and this etheric body we also possess an astral body—or whatever you would like to call it. This is the soul element proper in our make-up, and it is considerably more spiritual than the etheric body. During his period of physical development, the human being has by nature been more remote from this than from his etheric body, for the etheric body—underlying, as it does, the physical body—has a kind of picture form that is in perpetual motion, whereas the astral body is formless. If it is described in a picture, we know that this is only a way of representing it, for actually it is formless.

Over the last three or four centuries this astral body has been changing and is very different now. In the past, people's astral body was relatively full of spirituality; all kinds of spirituality flowed through it, and their spiritual feelings and motivations came from the spiritual qualities of the astral body. Today's astral bodies are empty, remarkably empty, and this is because the time has come for the spiritual world to reveal itself in full force, and human beings must be prepared to take this spiritual world coming from outside into themselves. It is to this end that astral bodies have gradually become empty. They are to be filled with what is being revealed from outside, and this affects the human being in a specific way. Which brings me to the symptom I said I wanted to point out. It is a fact that will sound quite strange when spoken of, just as strange as that melancholy expression on children's faces these days, but a fact nonetheless.

The most important event in the sequence that led to the outbreak of the World War calamity—so far as Berlin was concerned—took place on 1 August 1914 sometime between the afternoon and evening, between a quarter past three in the afternoon and eleven or twelve o'clock at night.[8] Various persons were involved, all of whom of course belonged to our materialistic times. For human souls today these are the most unfavourable hours for making decisions if those involved are basing them on materialistic considerations. We have entered an exceedingly important period of human evolution in which it is impossible for anyone to make a sensible decision unless he or she wakes up with it in the morning. This is true, however strange it may sound, and even external facts will increasingly show people how true it is. The person need not necessarily be conscious of having formed the decision, for it is in our subconscious that we live through what can be experienced the following day. We are not yet aware of this prophetic ability, but that is not the point I am making. If you entertain a thought at half past three, or at six o'clock, it may be a thought that you have already had in the night and now arises in you again. But as things stand for human beings today, if a thought arises which you have not already formed in the night but which is produced out of the events of the day, this cannot be a sensible thought. Today we are obliged to draw our most important motivations from the spiritual world. Such motivations do not come from the physical world at all. If we do not bring our decisions down with us, if we fail to draw on our links with the spiritual world, we cannot help being nonsensical.

The most essential things happen in our astral body at night when it is free of the physical and etheric body and has united with the spiritual world. To a greater extent than was the case with our ancestors it is prepared there for the good sense of the daytime. The moment of waking up after sleep should therefore be a holy one for modern human beings. We should feel how we have departed from the spiritual world and entered the physical. We should feel how everything good that makes us capable of acting sensibly has been obtained through our association with the spiritual world between going to sleep and waking up, through our association with the dead who were known to us in life but who have died sooner—in short, through what we experience when we associate in purely spiritual worlds with those who are no longer living in physical bodies. This experience in the spiritual world should generate in us a fundamental feeling for the holiness of the moment of waking up. By day this fundamental feeling will enable us in one instance to know that we are being helped by the spiritual world, and in another to know that no help is forthcoming, so that nothing must be decided until the following day.

This is how one leads one's life spiritually by genuinely reckoning with spiritual factors. However, people in these materialistic times do not reckon with spiritual factors, for they are always so 'clever'. They believe that nothing more than the instrument of the physical body is required in order to be clever. They do not call on what can come to them while they are separated from their physical body and associate with the spiritual world in their astral body. Nothing but the will to lead life in a spiritual way, the will to allow spiritual decisions, spiritual motivations to play a part in what we do in the physical world can make humanity truly healthy once again.

We ought to consider this very thoroughly today. The anthroposophical view of the world cannot mean that we absorb a number of abstract concepts which we regard as a kind of catechism to be sorted according to subject matter, and then rest content with having a world view different from that of other people. No indeed! The anthroposophical view of the world must be a matter of transforming our whole way of thinking and our whole way of feeling, so that a great moment of spiritual awakening comes about in us, telling us to let the spirit illumine our life through and through. Humanity's present misfortunes are the consequence of having taken to the extreme our rejection of the will to admit the spirit. Never has an event such as the present war calamity been brought about by such external, purely material causes. That is why it has become the most terrible calamity of all. We must learn from it that it was our former thinking, or former feeling and will that drove us into this calamity and that we shall not escape from it—although it will take on other forms—until we make the bold decision to embark on the inner transformation of our soul.

The facts I have been speaking about here are indeed facts: the melancholy expression on children's faces, the need to use our etheric body to gain an understanding of the world, and—with regard to our motivations of will—the need to turn, in the moment of waking up, to the remnant of our preceding sleep. For the future evolution of humanity it will be more and more necessary to listen to what the spirit has to tell us.

We shall have to realize that the anthroposophical view of the world is not intended as a source of something sensational for psychic idlers—and many present-day mystics are just that. It does not exist in order to supply the icing on the cake of life's outer, physical pleasures, for in fact it is deeply bound up with the profoundest motivations underlying our culture. We shall also have to realize that our culture cannot regain its health unless it is inspired by the anthroposophical view of the world. We should inscribe this fact in the depths of our soul once we have come to know this anthroposophical view.

Today I wanted to describe to you, from one point of view, the decisive moment in human evolution we have now reached. If we judge with the thinking now prevalent, it is of course quite easy to dismiss as mere foolishness the important things that are most in need of being said today. People consider themselves to be Christians but have not even understood the saying that what is wisdom with man is often foolishness before God, and that foolishness—perhaps folly and madness—before men can yet be wisdom before God.[9] People today so easily forget the inner motivations and like to cling to meaningless phrases. So long as you mention the word 'Christian', or 'Christ' or 'Jesus' after each fifth word, you are thought to be talking in a Christian sense, even if what you are saying is entirely unchristian. Yet when you intend to make known what the Christ today is revealing to souls, people regard you as unchristian if in doing so you include a

consideration of the words 'Thou shalt not take the name of
the Lord thy God in vain'—words that have, after all, been
accepted among the teachings of Christianity. Meanwhile
people who rattle off the Ten Commandments by rote, taking
the name of their Lord in vain at every moment, see themselves as especially Christian.

In similar fashion one is not regarded as a good German if
one does not have the word 'German' on one's lips all the
time. Yet today the most important thing is to realize how the
deepest resources of the German people have been as though
trampled underfoot over the last 30 years and need to be given
hope again through a deepening of spiritual life.

We look westwards and find there a cultural life that strives
to become completely materialistic, though it also possesses
an inner reliability of instinct to some degree, which will
prevent it from drowning in materialism. We look eastwards
and find there is a civilization that despises anything western,
including ourselves. This is because it still clings to an ancient
spirituality and is even renewing it in a certain way. Meanwhile here we stand in the midst and are called upon to find
the right path between the western materialism and that
eastern spirituality, the latter being, however, not wholesome
for ourselves. Here in the middle of Europe we ought to
become conscious of our great responsibility and conscious,
too, of how much we have lost this sense of responsibility over
recent decades. What has become of cultural life? It has
become an appendage of political life and economic life. As
the administrator of cultural life, the state has ruined it,
especially the education system. In its capacity of employer,
the economic life has ruined it further. What we need is a free
and independent cultural life, for only into a cultural life
which is free can we introduce what the spiritual world wants
to reveal to humanity. The wave of spirit must come down to

us. Yet it will never reveal itself to a civil servant, to a professor working for the state, to someone who in the cultural sphere is no more than a hired labourer of the economic life. It will only reveal itself to one who daily wrestles with cultural life, who has found his place fully within the free life of the spirit. Our time itself demands that we extricate the life of culture from the shackles of the state and of the economy.

These things, which are also being made known in another form today through our proposals concerning a 'threefold social ordering', are the Christianity of today; they are spiritual revelations clothed in external forms.[10] They are what humanity needs today. They alone offer us the realistic basis we need so urgently on which we can learn to transform our thinking.[11]

These are the things I wanted to speak about in a form in which it must appear today in face of contemporary events. Since we have once again had the opportunity to speak together here, I wanted to put this before your souls so that ever more and more and in ever wider and wider circles within our anthroposophical movement the endeavour might arise which can not only give the single individual an inner feeling of comfort but can also bear fruits for the cultural life of the whole of humanity.

It is deeply satisfying to see how many more friends of our anthroposophical movement are present today than were here a year ago. May the spirit now quickening the development of the world and of humanity bring it about that every year there may be as great, or even a much greater, increase in our numbers. For the more human souls there are who become convinced, by this spirit, of the need for the new thinking, feeling and will, and for a new sense of responsibility, the better it will be.

Notes

Lecture 1 (pages 3–26)

1 Lecture to members of the Theosophical Society, 'Über den Sinn des Lebens I', in *Christus und die menschliche Seele* (GA 155), Dornach 1994. The subject matter of this and the following Copenhagen lecture was also covered in 3 lectures in Nörrkoping (28, 29 and 30 May 1912), in *The Spiritual Foundation of Morality* (in GA 155), tr. M. Gardner, New York, Anthroposophic Press 1995. Lectures given in Kristiania (Oslo) during June 1912 are also available on this theme: *Man in the Light of Occultism* (GA 137), tr. not known, London, Rudolf Steiner Press 1964.

2 See R. Steiner, *An Outline of Esoteric Science* (GA 13), tr. C.E. Creeger, New York, Anthroposophic Press 1997, for a description of Atlantis, the Atlantean catastrophe and the seven post-Atlantean epochs of culture, the fifth of which is our present time. See also Roy Wilkinson, *Rudolf Steiner. Aspects of his spiritual world-view. Anthroposophy,* Vol. 1, London, Temple Lodge Publishing 1993.

3 The history and evolution of the earth and all its inhabitants is retained in the earth's etheric or life body. This 'Akashic Record' can be 'read' by someone who has acquired the necessary faculties. See R. Steiner, *Cosmic Memory* (GA 11), tr. R.M. Querido, New Jersey, Rudolf Steiner Publications 1971.

4 Raphael Santi or Sanzio (1483–1520), the great Italian painter.

5 Titian (*c.* 1489–1576), the greatest painter of the Venetian School.

6 Giovanni Santi (d. 1494).

7 Friedrich von Hardenberg (1772–1801), known as Novalis, German Romantic poet.

8 Reference not clarified.

Lecture 2 (pages 27–55)

1 Lecture to members of the Theosophical Society, 'Über den Sinn des Lebens II', in *Christus und die menschliche Seele* (GA 155), Dornach 1994. See Lecture 1, Note 1.

2 R. Steiner, *Knowledge of the Higher Worlds* (GA 10), tr. D. Osmond & C. Davy, London, Rudolf Steiner Press 1993, or *How to Know the Higher Worlds. A Modern Path of Initiation* (GA 10), tr. C. Bamford, Spring Valley, New York, Anthroposophic Press 1994.

3 For descriptions of Imagination, Inspiration and Intuition as further developments of the soul forces of thinking, feeling and will, see R. Steiner, *The Stages of Higher Knowledge* (GA 12), tr. L. Monges, F. Knight, New York, Anthroposophic Press 1967.

4 Lucifer and Ahriman were described by Steiner as powers who are opposed to proper human evolution. The former seeks to estrange human beings from the earth, the latter to enmesh them too firmly within it. See R. Steiner, *The Influences of Lucifer and Ahriman* (in GA 191 and 193), tr. D.S. Osmond, New York, Anthroposophic Press 1993.

5 Genesis 2:17 and 3:22.

6 For a description of the seven successive 'embodiments' of the earth, see R. Steiner, *An Outline of Esoteric Science*, op.cit.

7 R. Steiner, *Truth and Knowledge. An Introduction to Philosophy of Spiritual Activity* (GA 3), tr. R. Stebbing, New York, Steinerbooks 1981.

8 Reference not clarified.

9 See Note 6 above.

10 See Lecture 1, Note 2.

11 Angelus Silesius (1624–77), German religious poet. The quotation is from *Der cherubinische Wandersmann*.

12 R. Steiner, *Four Mystery Plays* (GA 14), tr. R. & H. Pusch, London, Rudolf Steiner Press 1997. The Soul's Probation, Scene 1.

13 Georg Christoph Lichtenberg (1742–99), German physicist and satirical writer.

14 Before parting from the Theosophical Society in 1913, Rudolf
Steiner used the terms 'theosophist' and 'theosophy', although
from the beginning he was speaking entirely in the light of his
own independent research into the spirit. He suggested that
the terms 'anthroposophist' and 'anthroposophy' should be
substituted in later editions of the lectures he had given prior to
that date.

Lecture 3 (pages 59–75)

1 Public lecture, 'Der Krankheitswahn' in *Die Erkenntnis der Seele
und des Geistes* (GA 56), Dornach 1985. The extant record of
this lecture (a longhand version made from the stenographer's
notes) is inadequate in places.

2 J.W. von Goethe, *Die Geheimnisse. Ein Fragment* (The Mysteries), 1984. Here translated by S. Kurland.

3 Heinrich Lahmann, founder of a therapy based on diet and
physical exercise by which he treated patients at his sanatorium
'Der Weisse Hirsch' near Dresden.

4 Moritz Benedikt, Viennese physician and anthropologist. The
examples are from his autobiography *Aus meinem Leben*,
Vienna 1906.

5 Rudolf Wagner, zoologist and physiologist. Carl Vogt, geolo-
gist and zoologist, author of *Köhlerglaube und Wissenschaft*
(Blind faith and science), Giessen 1855.

6 See Lecture 2, Note 14.

7 See Lecture 2, Note 3.

8 Plato, *Timaios*, Chapter VIII.

9 Aristotle (384–322 BC), *Poetics*.

Lecture 4 (pages 76–90)

1 Public lecture, 'Das Gesundheitsfieber', in *Die Erkenntnis der
Seele und des Geistes* (GA 56), Dornach 1985. See Lecture 3,
Note 1.

2 Ralph Waldo Trine (1866–1958), *In Tune with the Infinite*, New
York 1897.

3 J.W. von Goethe, introduction to 'Entwurf zu einer Farben-
   lehre' (Draft of a theory of colours) in his *Naturwissenschaftliche
   Schriften*, edited by Rudolf Steiner in Kürschner's *Deutsche
   National-Litteratur* (1884–1897), republished as GA 1a–3,
   Dornach 1975.
4 Luther is supposed to have said this.
5 Paracelsus (*c.* 1490–1541), German physician. Paraphrased
   quotation from P.R. Netzhammer, *Theophrastus Paracelsus.
   Das Wissenswerteste über dessen Leben, Lehre und Schriften* (A life
   of Paracelsus), Einsiedeln 1901).
6 J.W. von Goethe, *Primal Words: Orphic.* This translation by C.
   Middleton from *The Collected Works*, Vol. 1, *Selected Poems*, ed.
   C. Middleton, Princeton, New Jersey 1994.

Lecture 5 (pages 93–115)

1 Between 1903 and 1918 Rudolf Steiner gave 14 series of public
   lectures in Berlin. This lecture ('Das Glück—sein Wesen und
   sein Schein') is part of the ninth series *Menschengeschichte im
   Lichte der Geistesforschung* (GA 61), Dornach 1983.
2 Translator's Note: Translation of this lecture is made interesting by the fact that the German *Glück* means both 'good
   luck' and 'happiness', with the corresponding negative *Unglück*
   meaning (among other things) both 'bad luck' and 'unhappiness'. I have chosen to use mainly 'luck' (good or bad), but
   readers might like to play the game of substituting 'happiness'
   or 'unhappiness', which they will find fit the context in many
   instances.
3 Robert Hamerling (1830–89), Austrian poet. The essay 'Über
   das Glück' (Concerning luck) is in *Hamerlings sämtliche Werke*,
   Vol. 16, Leipzig, no date.
4 Giordano Bruno (*c.* 1548–1600), Italian philosopher of the
   Renaissance.
5 Diogenes 'the Cynic' (*c.* 412–323 BC), Greek philosopher and
   ascetic who lived in a tub. The single boon he craved from
   Alexander was that he would not stand between him and the

sun, to which Alexander replied: 'If I were not Alexander, I would be Diogenes.'

6   Jean Paul Friedrich Richter, usually called Jean Paul (1763–1825). Rudolf Steiner had written the introduction to a selection of his works in 8 volumes published in Berlin and Stuttgart by the Cotta'sche Buchhandlung in 1897. *Flegeljahre* (written in 1804) was partly translated as *Walt and Vult*, or *The Twins*, Boston, Mass., 1846.

7   Aristotle, in the first two books of *Ethics*.

8   Lecture of 23 November 1911 in R. Steiner, *Menschengeschichte im Lichte der Geistesforschung*, op. cit.

9   One of these, the lecture of 15 January 1912, is 'Christ and the Twentieth Century' in R. Steiner, *Spiritual History*, tr. W.F. Knox, London 1934.

10   The saying names 'stupidity' as the characteristic against which even the gods contend in vain.

11   J.G. von Herder (1744–1803), influential German writer.

12   J.W. von Goethe (1749–1832). The final lines of his poem 'Seefahrt' (Sea Voyage) have been more than a little adapted by Steiner here.

Lecture 6 (pages 116–145)

1   Lecture to members of the Anthroposophical Society, 'Wie kann die seelische Not der Gegenwart überwunden werden?', in *Die Verbindung zwischen Lebenden und Toten* (GA 168), Dornach 1995.

2   See Lecture 1, Note 2.

3   According to Rudolf Steiner, the human being is constantly developing and perfecting his physical as well as his higher principles. Whereas the intellectual or mind soul was worked on during the fourth post-Atlantean epoch, in the fifth epoch it is the turn of the consciousness soul.

4   See lecture 2, Note 4.

5   Lecture by F. Mahling on 23 September 1913, *Die Gedankenwelt der Gebildeten. Probleme und Aufgaben* (Concepts

entertained by educated people. Problems and tasks), Hamburg 1914. Quotations from pages 35 and 42.
6 See Lecture 2, Note 14.
7 R. Steiner, *Theosophy* (GA 9), tr. C.E. Creeger, New York, Anthroposophic Press 1994.
8 Even within Switzerland travel was difficult during the war.

Lecture 7 (pages 146–161)
1 Lecture to members of the Anthroposophical Society, in *Der innere Aspekt des sozialen Rätsels* (GA 193), Dornach 1989).
2 Vladimir Aleksandrovich Sukhomlinov, Russian foreign minister at the time of the outbreak of the First World War, in his memoirs (German 1924).
3 Henrik Ibsen (1828–1906), Norwegian dramatic and lyric poet. See for example *An Enemy of the People* (1882).
4 Björnstjerne Björnson (1832–1910), Norwegian poet.
5 Gerhart Hauptmann (1862–1946), German writer and dramatist. See *Die Weber* (The weavers).
6 Lecture 2, Note 3.
7 R. Steiner, *The Philosophy of Spiritual Activity: A Philosophy of Freedom* (GA 4), tr. rev. R. Stebbing, Forest Row, Sussex, Rudolf Steiner Press 1992.
8 See R. Steiner's Foreword to Helmuth von Moltke's pamphlet 'Die "Schuld" am Kriege', in *Light for the New Millennium*, ed. T.H. Meyer, tr. H. Herrmann Davey *et al.*, London, Rudolf Steiner Press 1997, p. 93.
9 1 Corinthians 3:19.
10 See R. Steiner, *Towards Social Renewal* (GA 23), tr. F.T. Smith, London, Rudolf Steiner Press 1977.
11 Speaking soon after the horrors of the First World War, Rudolf Steiner here turned to address his German audience so directly that for the purposes of this general volume the following three paragraphs have been included here in the Notes.

'We [in Germany] have had to wage war against a country that possesses an instinctive political life of great perfection, that has

long possessed many colonies and has an industrialism connected with these colonies. We fought as a country possessing
an industrialism that was only in its infancy and as one that was
only beginning to aspire to having colonies. We could have
done with genuine spirit for these endeavours. But no one has
sinned more against the spirit than have the leaders of the
economic life in Germany over the past three decades. Their
programme was: Reject the spirit and leave things to chance,
unspiritual chance. It is as though the world spirit had wanted
to teach the German people the greatest lesson by subjecting
them to the greatest test. This nation was to be shown that the
spirit cannot be ignored, and this nation will have to come to
the realization that the spirit can indeed not be ignored. Yet it
appears to be finding it difficult to learn this lesson, for it
remains inclined to condemn everything else except its own
lack of awareness of the need to be responsible towards the
spirit.

'The lamentable events occurring just now in this domain
show that people's souls are still asleep. There is a total lack of
awareness as to how ill-fitted for their task are the men who
guide the destiny of the German people and have to represent it
before the West just now. There is simply no realization that
the whole delegation to Versailles is senseless because of the
men taking part. The will not to examine events and see them
as they are still shows that people's souls are asleep, for
otherwise they would surely have pointed out by now that the
delegates to Versailles, whom we have sent, are as unfitted as
they possibly could be to understand the significance of the
present moment in world history. These things will only be
judged correctly when we become conscious of our responsibility towards the spirit, and once we recognize that we are
living in an extremely important moment of the world's history
in which it is our duty to take things very, very seriously.

'However much we repeat this, and repeat it again, it
remains of no avail, for people still find it easier to say that those
in charge are sure to see to things satisfactorily on our behalf.

But nothing good will result if those in charge persist in harbouring their old thinking and fail to turn to the new—whether they be long-standing aristocrats, or decadent aristocrats, or Marxist socialists who know nothing about the world apart from having absorbed some bits of Marx's *Kapital*, or anyone else. The revolution of 9 November 1918 was no revolution, for what has changed is only the superficial stucco. At best all that has changed is that new people now wear the superficial stucco previously worn by others. It is necessary to penetrate to the foundations of all this, but to do so one needs thoughts, and for these one must have good will, and this good will can only grow through being trained in active work with the spiritual world. This active work with the spiritual world is the sole real cure needed by humanity today.'

Note Regarding Rudolf Steiner's Lectures

The lectures and addresses contained in this volume have been translated from the German, which is based on stenographic and other recorded texts that were in most cases never seen or revised by the lecturer. Hence, due to human errors in hearing and transcription, they may contain mistakes and faulty passages. Every effort has been made to ensure that this is not the case. Some of the lectures were given to audiences more familiar with anthroposophy; these are the so-called 'private' or 'members' lectures. Other lectures, like the written works, were intended for the general public. The difference between these, as Rudolf Steiner indicates in his *Autobiography*, is twofold. On the one hand, the members' lectures take for granted a background in and commitment to anthroposophy; in the public lectures this was not the case. At the same time, the members' lectures address the concerns and dilemmas of the members, while the public work speaks directly out of Steiner's own understanding of universal needs. Nevertheless, as Rudolf Steiner stresses: 'Nothing was ever said that was not solely the result of my direct experience of the growing content of anthroposophy. There was never any question of concessions to the prejudices and preferences of the members. Whoever reads these privately printed lectures can take them to represent anthroposophy in the fullest sense. Thus it was possible without hesitation—when the complaints in this direction became too persistent—to depart from the custom of circulating this material "for members only". But it must be borne in mind that faulty passages do occur in these reports not revised by myself.' Earlier in the same chapter, he states, 'Had I been able to correct them [the private lectures], the restriction *for members only* would have been unnecessary from the beginning.'